Color of a Cry

Collection of Short Stories

Allen Goodson

Color of a Cry©

Copyright 2020 Allen Goodson

All Rights Reserved

This is in part a memoir. Some of the names have been changed to protect the identities of certain characters in the story.

Cover Design by Loretta Healy

Library of Congress Control Number: 2020904002

ISBN: 978-1-7347067-0-3

First Edition: March 2020

Please visit the author's website at: allengoodson.com

Printed in USA

Lava Tree Publishing

This book is a memoir of sorts.

Chapters 1-6 are stories of my youth and are true allowing for an aging memory. A memoir.

Chapter 7 is looking back. The story My Two Hearts doesn't belong there. Read it anyway.

Chapter 8 is fiction based on a one of a kind real life dog named Ike. RIP.

Chapter 9 is about change.

Some stories have been previously published:

Apa's
News and Farmer and Wadley Herald Newspaper
Macon Community News
Southland Magazine

CONTENTS

Prologue 1
Home

Chapter 1 Family and Place 7
Footsteps, Pawpaw, Dad, Mama, Sisters and Brother, Mama's Piano, Saturday Night Special.

Chapter 2 Early Years 31
Lobo, Fort Apache, Saturday Morning, Runaway Kid, Cow Pies, Doc, Lawrence Welk and Liver.

Chapter 3 Growing Up 51
Birds and Bees, Nekkid Statue, Giddy Up! What is that? Lessons of my Youth, Bovine Adventures.

Chapter 4 Perspective 67
Boys will be Boys, On Sunday, A Fair to Remember, Water, Black Eyed Peas, School Days, High Cotton, Nights Like This.

Chapter 5 Teenager 91
Higher Education, Almost Perfect, Glory, Glory to Georgia, Teen Driver, The Great Watermelon Caper, A Young Man's Spring.

Chapter 6 Coming Home 111
Coming Home, Southern Sailor, Color of a Cry, Mama's Closet, Time Gets Away.

Chapter 7 Visiting 127
Jefferson County, Visiting, Glory Days, A Man Remembered, My Two Hearts.

Chapter 8 Jake 145
Varmints, Jake and the Old Man, Jake's New Home, Jake Goes to Town, As It Should Be, A Time Remembered.

Chapter 9 Change 167
Death of a Family Farm, Harvest, Old Timer, Southern Fried.

Epilogue 179
Home Again

Prologue

Wadley, Georgia
Main Street 1949

Home

Home is where the heart is.
- Pliny the Elder, a Roman philosopher.

Folks generally agree with Pliny's sentiment. Home is more than a physical place. A home is a place where the heart goes for refuge and for comfort: a house, a cottage, an apartment. Some are nice and roomy; others are small. Each one is a place to rest your head, a place where your stuff is. I think most settle in one place for raising a family, for security, for comfort. However, none of that has ever been a serious concern for me. I have wandered, my heart content to move from place to place. When it was time to go, I went, with little worry of what I would do or where I would live when I got there.

But I once had a home for a long time, my childhood home. It is the one with memories I will never forget, no matter how long I live. Picture a white clapboard house with green trim. Picture two one-hundred-year-old cedar trees standing tall, shading a wide porch with rocking chairs, a swing and a sleeping dog. This house, a home for all of my youth, was surrounded by three hundred and sixty acres of rich farmland and woods, an incredible playground for a curious boy.

It sat at the intersection of two dirt roads. The unique location gave me and my childhood friend Bobby four distinctly different ways to go exploring. Mama didn't mind as long as we followed her rules: Be home by dark, don't come home wet, and don't get on any paved roads. We most often chose the northern artery, for it ran ten miles before meeting pavement, ten miles as a crow flies, but neither dirt roads nor young boys travel in straight lines.

Dirt roads follow the land, up hills and down into creeks and bottoms. They were usually just wide enough for two cars to pass.

Having no extra shoulders on the roads, the cars was either on the road or in the ditch. There were red clay hills that were slick in wet weather and sand beds that were traps in dry weather. At places, the roads went through open fields with crops on both sides. There were other places where the road was encroached on and seemingly swallowed up by the woods. The best places were the little wooden bridges that spanned streams or creeks, some with railings, and many without.

If we planned to be gone long, we would take food. Menu choices were biscuits, cookies, crackers, bologna, or peanut butter and jelly sandwiches. Luxury items when available were cake, cheese, sweet iced tea, or Kool-Aid in a mason jar. We never took water. If we got thirsty, it could be found along the way from a farmer's faucet, a cattle trough, or a running stream.

When there were working bikes, we rode; other times, we walked. We spent a lot of time trying to keep a couple of bikes in useable condition for our exploring. We fixed flats and we repaired chains. Sometimes we repaired brakes. Other times we rode with no brakes at all, which added an extra element of daring to our adventures.

We were always on the lookout for snakes and quicksand, our biggest worries, especially the two most deadly of all snakes, the Road Runner and the Coachwhip. I had been told a Road Runner was so fast he could catch you no matter how fast you were. I didn't know what a Coachwhip could do, but I didn't like the sound of it. Good luck must have been on our side, for we never saw either of those snakes. As for the quicksand, we never found ourselves drowning in it although that never stopped our concern.

Most of those roads I explored are gone now. The few red clay hills have been cut down, the sand beds covered over, and the wooden bridges long since replaced with modern concrete ones. Now the roads are wider; they have shoulders; they are paved with painted lines and traffic signs. Folks are in a hurry, and dirt roads aren't fast enough to get them there.

The house is still there, but it's just an old farm house worse for the wear. At one time, it was a new home for two young parents just starting out. Mom and Dad are gone now, too. We laid them to rest nearby. My sisters and I moved away years ago. Time has taken away nearly everything except the fond memories.

For me, this is a sad part of getting older. Gone are the days of childhood play, mama's love, and dad's helpful advice, but it's not all sad. All these years later, I still have memories. One remembrance triggers another and another and then I am home again, a farm boy eager to explore the roads and woods of the past, ever watchful for snakes and quicksand.

~1~
Family and Place

L-R John Franklin Goodson (Grandfather)
Ethel Myrick Goodson (Grandmother)
Gordon Myrick (Grandmother's Brother)
Standing: Mary Myrick (Grandmother's Mother)

Footsteps

The boy loved working with his father. It happened only when the work would accommodate him tagging along safely. The words, "Want to help?" thrilled him, made him feel important. He might not have any idea where they were going or what they would be doing, but what grown folks consider mundane is new and exciting to the young. And so it was with this kid. He thought his dad hung the moon.

He was a quiet boy, but when invited to help, youthful curiosity got the best of him.

"Where we going? "

"What we going to do?"

"Can Spider (his dog) go?"

His father gave short and often insufficient answers to his questions,

"You will see."

"We got work to do."

On this day the answer provided a bit more, "We going to the watermelon patch." This, of course, sparked the boy's curiosity even more.

"What we gonna do in the watermelon patch?"

"Are we going in the pickup truck?"

"Can I ride in the back?"

There were no answers forthcoming, so the boy tagged enthusiastically along behind his father. He had trouble keeping up due to his small stature and his father's long, deliberate stride. A short walk led them to the fertilizer shed behind their home where bags of fertilizer, each weighing one hundred pounds, were stored. The pickup, as if waiting for them, was parked there, tailgate lowered.

Wasting no time, his father began loading the heavy bags onto the truck bed. He watched his dad grab one, end to end, pick it up, turn, and load it on the truck. Seeing how it was done, he decided he should help. He put his arms on a bag but found his arms too short to reach end to end. He tried to pick it up another way, but he couldn't move it an inch. His father smiling, said to him, "I will do this; how about you run over to the tool shed and get us a foot tub?"

The boy, suddenly feeling a sense of pride with a task he could do, took off running toward the shed. He knew what a foot tub was; he had helped fill them before with vegetables from the garden. When he got there, there were two. One was half full of fresh dug new potatoes; one was empty. Which one? His father hadn't said. He took a wild guess, grabbed the empty one, and ran back to where his father had finished loading the truck. Spider had come out from under the house to see what was going on. His father took the foot tub from the boy's hands, set it in the back of the truck beside the fertilizer and said to the boy, "Good job, jump in."

"The back?" the boy asked.

His father nodded his head. The boy was thrilled, helping his dad and riding in the back of the truck all the same day.

His father got in, pulled away from the barn, and headed down the dirt road to the watermelon patch. Spider, following just behind the slow-moving vehicle, had no problem keeping up. The boy called out to his furry friend, "Come on boy! Run, Spider, run!" It doesn't get better than this, a boy, his faithful companion, and dad. The ride to the patch ended far too soon or so he thought.

When they stopped, his curiosity struck again and he begin to wonder what his job would be now that they were there. He watched his father walk to the back of the truck, set the foot tub on the ground, stand a bag of fertilizer on its end, tear it open, lift it, and fill the foot tub. The boy had no idea how to help and asked, "What you want me to do?" His father picked up the tub full of fertilizer, cradled it in the crook of his left arm, smiled at the boy and said, "Follow me and make sure I do it right." The comment was a puzzle to the boy but at an even younger age he had learned to do as his father asked. So he did.

His father began walking down the rows, reaching in the foot tub for fertilizer and throwing a handful by each newly sprouted watermelon plant. The boy trailed behind, not sure of his job, but enjoying the company of his father and Spider, who had taken the first opportunity to lie down under and in the shade of the pickup. It was mesmerizing to watch his father. There was a rhythm to his work, a steady stride, a reach for fertilizer, and a timely toss. Never a misstep, machine like, but with a touch only farmers know.

Soon they came to the end of a row and his father walked towards the truck. The boy asked, "Are we done?" "No," his father replied, "I need more fertilizer."

His father did the same as before; he filled the tub, picked it up and said to the boy, "How am I doing?" The boy wasn't expecting the question and was unsure of what to say. The fact is he looked up to this man, wanted to please him, and replied as his father had said to him earlier, "Good job."

Up and down the rows they went. The boy began to get bored watching his father and fell behind. Several times he had to run to catch up. Instead of watching his father's work, his eyes wandered. Looking down, he saw a long line of man-sized footprints in the soft loamy sand. He attempted, as boys will, to match those steps, but they were too far apart for his short legs. Failing to match his dad's stride and suddenly without knowing, he set a life goal for himself that is among the hardest to live up to. He thought, when I get big, when I grow up, I can walk in those steps.

This short story is a memory not forgotten. That small boy, now grown, has learned the footsteps of his dad, a humble and honest man, are still hard to fill.

Pawpaw

I have no memory of the man though he played an influential role in my being. He was one who made my life's journey easier because of who he was and how he lived. I did meet him, but try as I might, I can find no recollection of him. I must have heard his voice and seen his smile, but I was little more than a baby when he passed. His name was John Franklin Goodson, and he was my paternal grandfather.

Born in Allendale, South Carolina, on October 17, 1884, he married the prettiest girl in town in 1912, and they moved to Millhaven, Georgia. That was only twenty-five miles southwest of his home town, not far even in those days, though the move involved taking a barge across the Savannah River. He'd found work there managing a cotton plantation. I can only imagine that to be a wonderful time in his life, a young newlywed with a good job, and soon-to-be father of his first two children, Willie and Frances.

He couldn't have known at the time, but trouble loomed on the horizon. Years earlier, when he was just a boy, a small insect that would eventually have a huge impact on his new life in Georgia crossed the Rio Grande River between Mexico and Texas. The scientific name for the vermin responsible for that impending disaster is Anthonomus grandis, commonly known as the boll weevil. It's a fact that the first boll weevil crossed the river near Brownsville, Texas, in 1892 and made its way to Alabama by 1909. Traveling up to one hundred sixty miles per year, it traversed the South and soon made its way to Millhaven. The boll weevil destroyed the cotton industry, and this young father lost his job when the plantation could no longer afford to pay him.

Fortunately, he found a farm for sale some sixty miles southwest of Millhaven near a small town called Wadley, and they moved. Soon after that, two more children came along, Dorris and Emmett.

All the while, he worked the farm raising chickens, pigs, and cows. He planted corn and winter grains to feed them. He also ran a small store where he sold all manner of goods to the nearby neighbors, including his annual harvest of watermelons for which he became famous. He sold watermelon seeds to growers in Florida, and he grew sugar cane and made syrup. He also had the only pear orchard I ever saw in the South.

Years after he was gone, I spent the Sunday afternoons of my youth exploring that place. The barns and outbuildings were meticulously built with an eye for detail. The weathered boards had been cut precisely and fit together perfectly. In one open shed with a wood-shingled roof, a giant black iron metal pot sat waist high on rows of red brick. Underneath was a space for a fire to cook the sugar cane juice and attached was a tall chimney of the same brick to take the smoke away. The pear orchard grew on the west side of the house and was responsible for many belly aches from eating too many green pears. A row of pecan trees lined the roadway in front of his home and three more parallel rows continued back toward the fields, shading the barns where he worked. Four magnolia trees surrounded and cooled the house.

I loved to crawl under his home to stir the dirt and to sing for doodlebugs, a game played by children of the South. "Doodlebug, doodlebug, come out your hole; your house is on fire, and your children will burn." If you were lucky, out came a doodlebug. I played cowboys and Indians with cousins in those barns. I imitated TV western heroes of the time, Roy Rogers, Hopalong Cassidy, and the Lone Ranger. Hemmed up in the hay loft from a surprise attack, using feed sacks for cover and my hands for six shooters, I fought off war party after war party that my vivid imagination dreamed up.

On the east side of the house was a portico with two white columns, a trellis of roses filled the opening between the columns, and two concrete strips for tires that would carry a car from the road right up to the front stoop. I thought those concrete strips were the coolest thing I had ever seen. The craftsmanship of his buildings, the rows of pecan trees, the rare pear orchard, and the unusual paved strips of his driveway made me realize that there was more to this man than just being an ordinary farmer.

To his family, he was "Pawpaw." I wish I could see him now. I'd enjoy his smile and sit and talk with him. I'd like to shake his hand, man to man. I'd like to tell him I'd admired what he had built and I'd thank him for his good name, and his children's good name, for it has given me advantages that I did nothing to earn. I'd also like to talk with him about the boll weevil, that little pesky insect that caused him and other Southerners so much trouble. And finally, I'd ask him if I could thank that boll weevil, for that's how I came to be born in Wadley, his final resting place and the beloved home of my youth.

Dad

He grew up on a small farm a few miles east of Wadley during the 1920's and 30's. There were no school buses. He, his sister, and two brothers walked to school every day. At times there was a cart and a horse to make the trip easier. In his early years, weather permitting, he went to school barefoot. His sixth-grade teacher, who also happened to be mine many years later, said he had been a very good student. She said I had a lot to live up to. After high school, he attended the University of Georgia. I never asked him if he ever dreamed of being anything but a farmer, but like his father before him, that is what he became. However, in my eyes he was more.

The buildup to war interrupted his college. He joined the Navy. I should have asked him why; perhaps he wanted to see the world, a country boy from southeast Georgia being curious about what's out there. He was at Pearl Harbor when it was attacked and spent the remaining part of the war on board ship patrolling the Aleutian Islands. He served his country for over five years without complaint. For that he should have received a medal. In my eyes he was a hero.

After the war, he came home and married a young widow with two small girls. Within a year I came along, a year and a half later my baby sister was born. To support his wife and four children, he carried mail on a rural route and farmed in the afternoon. After a few years he managed to drop the mail route and farm full time. He was a good farmer blessed with an innate ability to grow nearly anything and a work ethic that encouraged him to work long days. In my eyes he was more: he was a man to admire.

He wasn't a hard man with discipline. I don't ever recall a lecture. My youthful failings were corrected with few words, often just "No," or if my behavior had been beyond acceptable, a stern and disgusted, "Boy." Sometimes he would add a head shake, as if he couldn't believe what I had done. It was enough to get his message across. I would argue with Mama, but never with Dad. I have made many mistakes in my life, but rarely have I felt more ashamed than when I disappointed my father. He was a humble man of few words, but he was more: he was kind.

His sense of humor was understated but very much alive if you knew him. Jackie Gleason broke him up. Don Adams of "Get Smart" with his shoe phone was a favorite. "Clown" was a word he used to describe people with a zest for life or politicians he had no use for, as in, "They are a bunch of clowns." One of his favorite jokes went like this: A lady opens her refrigerator and a rabbit is sitting on the shelf. Lady asked the rabbit, "What are you doing in my refrigerator?" Rabbit says, "What kind of refrigerator is this?" Lady says, "It's a Westinghouse."

Rabbit says, "I'm just westing." He was a gentle, fun-loving man.

I was in my twenties and farming with Dad before I ever heard him utter a four-letter word. I was growing into a man and he treated me as one. When younger I did as Dad asked, but now we discussed farming plans and problems. No matter how off the wall my ideas sounded, he never dismissed them without offering back sound advice. When my ideas were good, he encouraged me. We occasionally had a beer or drink together. The troubles of life seemed to roll off him. Like most of us he wasn't a perfect man, but his steady and practical approach to life appealed to me. He was a thoughtful, rational thinking man, but in my eyes, he was more: he was a friend.

After his retirement in the late 80's, he came to Maui and spent a couple of months with me. We sat as men on my lanai every evening, sharing a beer, watching the tide roll in and the sun setting over the West Maui channel with the islands of Molokai and Lanai in the distance. We didn't talk much, just as it had been when we sat together on the porch of a Georgia farm house twenty something years earlier and listened to the sounds of the night. He enjoyed the still of the night as I now do. I am my father's son. He was a quiet man, but in my eyes, he was so much more than that. He was DAD.

Too many Father's Days have come and gone without him. What I wouldn't give to sit on the porch with him again and listen to the night. Sadly, life doesn't work that way. If you still have your father, go see him this weekend; if you can't go, call him, before time gets away. I wish I could call mine.

Mama

I don't know how she raised us. I mean where did the patience come from? Where did the knowledge how to come from? We were four children, three girls and tow-headed me, a boy and middle child. Of course, my sisters, if you hear them tell it, were perfect angels who wanted to grow up to be princesses. And they did, every one of them. But because of their good behavior in our youth I heard often, "Why can't you be like your sisters?"

Over the years Mama tried different ways to correct my poor behavior. Early on, she often threatened me with, "If you don't straighten up and fly right, I'm going to snatch a knot in you." Some moms, I hear, said "jerk a knot in your tail," but mine was seriously committed to "snatching knots." These words meant simply, mind me NOW, as they came after several previous warnings of "don't do that" or just plain "stop!" Now years later when I have an ache or pain, I wonder if it might be a residual effect from being snatched into knots as a young boy. Probably not, it's more likely just old age.

When I turned ten, she changed to, "It's for your own good." As in, "Eat your liver; it's for your own good." It might have been but I'll never know. I hated liver, still do. The ultimate threat was always, "If you don't straighten up, I will tell your father." I didn't like those words, so I did as she asked, mostly. I was also concerned she might go back to snatching knots and I liked those even less.

During my teenage years, she discovered "restriction" which, when imposed, meant, I was stuck on the farm. I still went to school and church, but that wasn't a perk as I saw it. Missing either of these was sometimes what had landed me on restriction in the first place. I tried to bust out a few times, but my sisters squealed on me. I was captured and returned to solitary confinement by her deputy, who was also Dad. It was a good thing she was a forgiving woman and, more often than not, commuted my sentences. Otherwise, I would still be serving time today, some fifty years later.

As people grow older, they gain a better appreciation for their parents; this is especially true with me. Mom was born in 1928 and spent her entire youth in the worst years of the Great Depression. She was one of a family of five girls, raised by a single mom. My mother's young life was arduous, yet I rarely heard her complain. She enjoyed life, except possibly times when a troublesome towheaded little boy, me, drove her crazy.

How did she do it, all the work it took to raise four kids? How any woman does that is beyond my comprehension. We lost her few years back; she had been a sister, a daughter, a wife, a mother, eighty-four years of life. Her once towheaded boy stood graveside with a lump in his throat, tears in his eyes, and regrets in his heart. I should have called more, visited more, told her I loved her more - should've, should've, should've.

As a man of sixty plus years, far from perfect, I still need an occasional knot snatched in me. She knew when I needed it most and it was always for my own good.

Sisters and Brother

Older sister, older sister, me, baby sister, or girl, girl, boy, girl made up my family not counting Mom and Dad. It was the glory days of the fifties, of one phone, one-bathroom homes. With three females, four counting Mama, the use of either remained troublesome my entire youth.

My sisters shared a large bedroom with three beds, two dressers, multiple night stands, and a single closet. The room was painted pink or purple or baby blue at one time or another. Imagine the painting and furniture moving that went on over the years. It's a female thing.

In fact, about the only time I was allowed in their room was when they wanted to move furniture.

"Allen, can you help us move the beds?"

"Why?"

"We need them on this other side."

"Why?"

"Because."

"Because why?"

"Why do you ask so many questions?" one exasperated sister asked.

"Because."

"Because Tom might ride by and we want to see his car lights."

Who cares?

They did. Young love, there was no reasoning with it. I had a bedroom to myself. In eighteen years, I never once moved the furniture.

They had a phonograph that played 45's. For the uninformed,

or anyone under forty, 45's are single song records with a hit tune on one side and something lesser on the other. Seven inches in diameter, each with a hole in the center larger than a silver dollar, they sold at Woolworths and other fine stores for ninety-nine cents plus tax back when a dollar was worth something and hard to come by.

My oldest sister was obsessed with Elvis. Because of her obsession, the lyrics of "Love Me Tender" are imbedded in my brain. She was a music groupie before they were called that. In August 1977, I found myself in the hospital with a broken leg. The reason I was there should not be printed in a family newspaper. Nevertheless, when my older sister stopped by for a visit the next morning, she was crying. Being the sensitive, understanding type, I told her, "Don't cry. It's all right, I will be fine."

To which she replied, "I ain't crying about you; Elvis died."

Ah, sisterly love.

The middle sister was not into pop music, but she was very much into being a majorette, generally, a quiet activity except when practiced in the house. The kerplunk with every drop of the baton was a constant and annoying sound on the scale of "Excedrin headache number seven." Dad and Mom allowed this in-house practicing but, to their credit, stopped her in her tracks when she asked about using fire batons. The local volunteer fire department equipment was antiquated and their success in saving country homes was poor at best.

My baby sister brought loud music back with vengeance. The older sisters had grown and left home. She had the bedroom and phonograph to herself. It was by then the mid-sixties, when teenage girls described their favorite musicians as "dreamy." For some reason, unbeknown to me, she fell in love with "Cherish" by the Association. The lyrics went:

Cherish blah, blah, blah

Cherish blah, blah, blah

Cherish blah, blah, blah

Cherish blah, blah, blah

And on and on which I heard over and over, ad infinitum. My lyrics went, "That's seventy-eight times in a row, for Christ's sake, turn it off!"

I didn't really use "for Christ's sake" in my retort. If I had, my Southern Baptist mother would have sent me to the front yard to fetch a switch from the all-too-convenient crepe myrtle that grew there. I shouldn't have to tell school boys of the era, the aforementioned shrub has lovely flowers with supple, thumb-thick stems and served as a handy educational tool for mamas everywhere. Flowers aside, this might well have been the primary reason for their popularity.

That single room my sisters shared was woefully short of closet space; old houses weren't built with much. On the other hand, who builds any room with enough closet space for three females? Being a curious boy, I snuck in their closet one evening and found forty dozen pairs of shoes and about the same number of dresses. I got tangled up with a poodle skirt and missed supper. Mom and Dad were just before calling the sheriff and filing a missing son report when I managed to stumble out.

The bathroom, or rather the use of it, was real a problem. To make matters worse, these were literally big hair days. Bouffant, they called it. While I am not sure that is the correct name for the style, I am sure they created the first holes in the ozone layer with their obscene use of hair spray. A person could choke to death if he entered the room too soon. Every morning and every night there was a parade of females in and out, in and out. I would try to rush in when I reached the point of "really got to go." "Mama, Allen is in the bathroom, and I have to roll my hair!" God forbid she didn't get her hair rolled, can't have Luke seeing her with unrolled hair. I went outside. It was simpler.

It was worse with the phone. There was only one. It was attached to the kitchen wall where phones are supposed to be. If it rang, you knew right where to find it. If you went somewhere, the phone stayed at home till you got back. It was a simpler world. No matter, I needed a Declaration from Congress, plus a court order, to use it.

"Mama, tell Allen I am talking to Steve right now, and he can use the phone when I am through." "When I am through" meant next Tuesday. Eventually dad got an extension put in their room. He, too, had grown tired of hearing endless conversations like,

"You hang up."

"No, you."

"No, you."

"You first."

"Blab, blab, blab.........blab, blab."

It was enough to make you sick.

I joke around. My sisters are all grown up now, but I dare not mention ages except to say they are mostly thirty-nine. They are fine women and have become moms and grand moms. Even though I teased and harassed them throughout our youth, they have since forgiven me and accepted me as I am. I still tease them unmercifully, but the truth is, I would be a lesser man without my three lovely sisters and the experience of growing up together. Blessings come in many packages. Some have small closets, talk endlessly on the phone, and act like girls. That, folks, is a good thing.

Mama's Piano

Mama loved piano music. Born in 1928, one year before the Great Depression, and raised Southern Baptist, she grew up with the music of her faith, worship service after worship service, Sunday after Sunday. She was a devoted Baptist for life and knew the hymnal backward and forward. She did her best to pass this love on to her children.

Sunday mornings on the way home from church, she drove me and my three sisters crazy. The song choice would be whatever had just been sung during the morning worship. "How Great Thou Art" was a favorite. Neighborhood dogs barked when we drove by. I am not saying her singing was bad, but we weren't interested in hearing it at all. During the warm months and with no air conditioning in the car, we could roll down the windows, thereby getting a measure of relief as the wind and road noise helped drown her out. During the cold months, we were captive to her vocals. My sisters did eye rolls; I used fingers to plug my ears.

This passion of hers prompted the purchase and surprise appearance of a full size, well-used, upright piano in our living room. It, along with a round spinning piano stool, was placed near the twenty-three-inch black and white, top of the line at the time, Motorola TV. I should mention to the young readers, TV's of the day were poor quality and would make you go blind if you sat too close, at least it was so according to Mama.

With the addition of the piano, the entertainment center for the Goodson family had grown considerably during the few hours I had been at school that day. Mama, bless her heart, hoped that one of her children had a talent for playing. The fact that my father's oldest brother made his living teaching music and was a talented player only encouraged her. Uncle Willie lived in Atlanta but came home often. On these visits, he would sit and play Baptist hymnals continuously and without sheet music. Mama was in heaven while she hummed and sang along. My sisters found peace in their room, which was located at the back of the house and farthest from the racket. Rarely being permitted into their room, I was left to escape on my own. If the weather was good, no problem. I had access to a three hundred and sixty-acre farm and untold opportunities to find trouble or for it to find me. If the weather was poor, I was trapped. The long version of "Whispering Hope" played by Uncle Willie was torture. Allan Sherman's "Hello Muddah, Hello Faddah" was more to my taste.

After neither of my two older sisters became pianists, the task fell to me. I can't say I enjoyed it at all. I was to take lessons from Mrs. Brim. A sweet lady of many talents, she was a substitute school teacher, the piano player at church, and a columnist for the local newspaper, *The News and Farmer* and *Wadley Herald*. Her weekly column kept our citizens up-to-speed with whose house had been painted, who had entertained out of town guests, early azalea blooms spotted around town, and the like. She reported on shut-ins as well: "Mrs. Beulah Mae Tidwell is down with the misery, calls are appreciated."

The piano lessons were scheduled during the school day and, much to my regret, during the recess after lunch. All my friends were on the playground doing what kids do, which is what I wanted to do, but I found myself sitting at a piano, pounding away, and receiving colored stars after each day's lesson. The color depended on my success or lack thereof. To her credit and my good fortune, deservingly so or not, Mrs. Brim was fast and loose with the gold stars.

Months went by and I made progress, poor progress but progress. Enough so that after a consultation between Mama and Mrs. Brim, it was decided I was ready for the big time, that being the afternoon meeting of the Baptist Ladies Missionary Circle. In this life, I have been more nervous one other time -- during an IRS audit.

The performance required a haircut, taking a bath in the middle of the day, washing my rusty elbows three times, and putting on

Sunday-go-to-meeting clothes. One other thing, the song selected was "Whispering Hope." Obviously, I wasn't involved with that decision. Cleaned up and dressed for Sunday school, on a beautiful weekday afternoon fully made by the Man Upstairs for outdoor play, I was led into the church and introduced. I didn't know why because every woman there knew my life history, forward, backward, and in between. It was a small town.

In front of a couple dozen women, dressed in their Sunday best, most with coiffed blue hair, and all sincerely dedicated to the missionary's plight, I sat down at the piano scared to death and played the worst rendition of "Whispering Hope" known to man. After it was over, I was rewarded with a polite round of applause, indicating appreciation of my effort if not the quality. I escaped as quickly as possible to our family car outside, miserable with where I was, but glad it was over, and waited on Mama.

As bad as it all seemed to me at the time, I learned two things about pianos. I learned that a piano needed to be tuned. Two men came all the way from Augusta, an hour's drive away, to tune the piano. What was fascinating to a young farm boy was that the tuner was blind. I couldn't imagine such a thing. I assumed this tuning would help my playing, but it didn't.

Along with my playing, I also learned a round piano stool could be used as an amusement ride. One evening after supper when the family had settled down and gathered in front of the TV, I lay across the stool. Dad was watching Jackie Gleason and whenever Jackie let out a bellow, Dad would laugh. I didn't get the humor, was bored, and began to entertain myself on the piano stool by spinning round and round, faster and faster. Not amused by my disturbance, Dad simply said, "Stop." I ignored his command. He was a fair man but had no patience for hard headed boys who didn't listen and was not in the habit of issuing multiple warnings. Without me knowing, he took off his belt. Then he gave me a good one on the place God intended you to get a good one, not an unusual event with a boy and his dad, except that his belt broke in two. The lick he had administered was mild, but his worn and weathered belt wasn't up to the task. The story has been repeated many times in our family and, exaggerated as we do with childhood stories, told of how one night Dad broke his belt using it on my posterior. We laugh and laugh.

Truth is, I have no talent for music. Soon after my one and only public performance, Mama let me quit. Funny how it goes, a piano one day made a Mama proud of her boy and another day, a Dad mad. This is not an earth-shaking story but a priceless memory for me. Years later as a grown man I asked one of those church ladies if she remembered me playing "Whispering Hope." She paused a moment as if thinking her answer through, smiled the kindest smile, was brutally honest and said, "Allen, it was the worst rendition I ever heard, but you were so cute, bless your heart, and you tried your best."

Life is a pile of memories and the older you are the bigger the pile. If I had been any good at playing the piano, the church lady possibly would have forgotten my performance. But she didn't. She remembered with a heartfelt smile, as do I.

Saturday Night Special

It was the usual Saturday night. My three sisters and I were up after nine watching Gunsmoke; mom and dad had since retired for the evening. Dad almost always went to bed at nine; mama sometimes stayed up with us kids, but on this night she chose the earlier hour.

Our home had an open porch across the entire front of the house and on the porch sat rocking chairs and a porch swing. The porch light at our home remained on every night until Dad went to bed. He was a stickler about not wasting electricity, or anything else for that matter, and each night before retiring, he turned off the lights not needed. That was most of them. Besides, it was 1961, a farm home in the country and late for those times. No guests were expected unless someone's car was stuck in a ditch or broken down near our place.

My sisters sat on the living room couch that backed up to windows facing the porch. As usual I sat inches from the TV, ignoring mama's constant warning that this would cause me to go blind. I am happy to report today my eyesight is good although, once a person is years past the half century mark, things do look blurry now and again, a malady related to my age rather than to a poor habit from my youth.

On this night, I was sitting in front of the TV, eyes glued to Gunsmoke and Miss Kitty, a fine looking woman and considered a good one even though she ran a saloon, when out of nowhere one of my sisters let out a scream and exclaimed, "There's a man on the porch!"

I jumped up from in front of the TV, ran to look out the window and saw a man sitting in one of the rocking chairs, seemingly comfortable, rocking away.

I dashed from the living room across the hall and knocked on my parent's door. Without waiting for a response, I burst into their bedroom frantically announcing a man was on the porch. I hadn't said it nor had my sister said it, but it was a colored man. Let me stop here for a minute and explain, "colored" was the politically correct word of the time. In 1961 it wasn't a word that was meant to be disrespectful; there were other words for that.

Dad jumped out of bed, pulled on a pair of pants, walked into the hall barefoot, turned on the porch light and went outside. I could hear mumbling but couldn't make out any of the conversation. After a minute or so, Dad came back in, grabbed shoes, a shirt, and the handgun he kept in his dresser drawer. By this time, Mama had gotten up and huddled us children together in the living room, I suppose protecting us in the only way she knew how. The TV had been turned off.

We could see through the window what was happening outside. Dad waved the gun at the man and marched him out to the dirt road in front of our house. He then got in the car and drove along behind as the man walked down the road toward town and away from our home.

As it was happening the incident was scary, but in the end, it turned out to be not much. I heard Dad say the word "drunk" to Mama after it was over. I also heard him say the man's name and, though I was young, I knew him and thought him to be a good man. Apparently, alcohol caused him to make a poor decision that night. Today, as a man now older than my father was at the time, I understand that people make mistakes.

I can report this was the only time I saw my father threaten a living creature and, other than fish, I never saw him kill one. Though he owned a handgun and a shotgun, the only times he ever fired either was at crows in the watermelon patch or blackbirds in the cornfield. Even then, he shot more to scare them off than to harm them. The times farm animals needed putting down he always got someone else to do the job. He didn't hunt.

On this night he was calm yet stern with the impaired visitor, doing all that was needed to protect his family. Others may have acted harsher. In this life, we choose our way. Dad chose firm, though quiet and respectful. It's how he lived.

2

Early Years

My Sister Laura and Me

Lobo

Young children view life from a different perspective than adults do. My dad, mom, and three sisters were an integral part of my daily life, but most of my pleasure and enjoyment came from other things. It may not be that way for all children, but it was for me in 1959. I was ten years old, and my pals, my Lionel train, and my dog were the things that made life complete and good.

The Lionel train had been from Santa the Christmas before. One so blue it hurt your eyes, it was exactly what I had asked for. If there is a better feeling of excitement and joy than a young child's on Christmas morning, I don't know what it is. I would love to see a video of me finding that wished for, hoped for gift from Santa under the tree. My step grandfather (Mr. Lonnie, we called him) built, from a four by eight sheet of plywood, a fold down table in my bedroom. I secured the tracks on it in a rectangular circle, painted green for grass. I laid out a "Y" shaped road for cars and trucks inside the tracks and painted it gray. It was a job well done considering my age. My friends and I spent hours of enjoyment while this train made the journey round and round.

My dog Lobo was a German shepherd. He was a gift from my first cousin, who lived in town. As it turned out, close neighbors and a big barking dog don't mix. The cousin had named him Lobo, which means "wolf," and was fitting since he looked like one.

Lobo and I were free to roam the farm and we did, together and often. If you saw me, you saw Lobo. Dogs provide companionship and a love that is more suitable for a young boy to my way of thinking. With a mom and three sisters, there was too much of the mushy, mushy female kind around. Lobo's kind was perfect.

A young boy couldn't have asked for more; it was as good as life could be. Then one day Lobo growled and snapped at one of my sisters, something he had never done. It was determined he had contracted rabies. He would have to be put down. Late that afternoon dad made us all go inside and I heard the boom, boom of a gun. There was no mention of the day's events at the supper table that night. Knowing something and believing it are two different things. The next morning, I ran out to look for Lobo. He was nowhere to be found.

A mistake has been made about humans and dogs. Humans have a life expectancy of seventy-five years; dogs have one of fifteen years. If I designed the "master plan," the life expectancies of both would be similar. We would have them for longer. Dogs have earned that; humans, I am not so sure of.

Fort Apache

I don't know what it was with young boys in my day, but we were obsessed with forts. Every friend had one at some point. Maybe it's because of the cowboy shows we watched, or just the early beginnings of the desire that all human beings have: a place of their own, a place of refuge, a place for their stuff. Or maybe it's just the wonderful imagination of youth. Whatever it is, my pal Bobby and I built several over the years.

Some were holes in the ground covered with sheets of tin, while others were simple lean-to's, wood planks laid against tree limbs. We built them from hay bales stored in the barn lofts on the farm, but our very finest one had wood walls and a wooden roof. Building forts was limited to materials available and there were limits to materials we were allowed, limits imposed by my parents. As with most things in those days, waste was avoided at all cost and in their eyes, forts were certainly nonessential. Go figure the adult mind. If this hadn't been the case, we would have built many more.

During inclement weather we built them inside, but these forts were less fun and short-lived. We couldn't light candles and, worse we had to keep the noise down. Otherwise, there would be issues with the woman of the house, namely Mama, who frequently took aversion to the loud repetition of our imaginary six shooters and Indian war cries, and especially the use of her good blankets for the construction.

Sisters presented other problems with inside forts. I had three, sisters, not forts. With a fort deep in the woods, they pretty much stayed away, afraid of snakes, bugs, and poison ivy. Inside was just too convenient for them. They would come into my room and want to play. We had a standard rule: no girls allowed, which of course made them mad, which led to fussing and a lot more noise. Sometimes we would give in and tell them if they knew the password, we would let them in. Why they couldn't remember "Geronimo," I will never know. This led to more noisy fussing, which also upset Mama.

My mother was a short-legged woman, but when she had had enough she could get those legs going like a blitzing linebacker, rush in my room, grab our fort blanket, fold it up, and have it back in the linen closet before you could say "Dale Evans." She would have run us out the house, as well, but the only reason we had an inside fort to begin with was bad weather.

The finest fort we ever built was in the woods across the dirt road in front of our house. There wasn't much underbrush, so we could explore it easily. It was the perfect spot for a fort. Just out of these woods towards town was a narrow open field, which was actually a cleared easement for power lines, then another narrow strip of woods, and then a twenty-five-acre field with a tenant house sitting next to a dirt road. Dad rented this house out or offered it as a perk to get farm help.

One day when no one was living there, Bobby and I went in. We took note of several interior doors that would make a fine fort with minimal work. Further, they would be easy to take down, since simple pins held them to hinges. The location was close to our preferred building site, so moving them would not be a problem. Also, we would be hidden from view, an ideal situation with commandeered building materials.

In addition to the interior house doors we also "borrowed" the door from the two-seater privy out back. For those who may not know, a two-seater was considered high end in the day and only out-done by a brick one. Here I have to admit that I never saw a brick one. (I had heard older boys compliment girls by saying they were built like one. I met girls like that when I grew older.)

I wish you could have seen that fort. Square as can be with hardly a bent nail, it even had a skylight in the shape of a quarter moon. The outhouse door had made a fine roof. On completion we moved in, fought off Indians and bad guys, made all the noise we wanted, and my sisters stayed away. It was heaven on earth.

Then, one evening a few days later, just before supper, dad walked in the house, looked at me, and said, "Where my doors, boy?" with emphasis on the word "boy." He was a man of few words, but with those four words and his look, the message was clear enough. I was busted.

Do you know how many hours it takes chopping cotton and toting watermelons to pay for your sins of commandeering doors from a tenant house? I don't remember for sure, but it was a lot and I never "borrowed" a house door again. I say that now, but if I were ten again, who knows? There is something special about a fort and a young fella's imagination.

Saturday Morning

"Deep in the heart of the Zambezi jungle, there lives a man who knows no fear of the wild animals and dangers that lurk in every direction. His name is Bwana John."

This was the opening to Bwana John, a TV show hosted by a local newscaster dressed in safari attire. Most of the show was a Tarzan movie, which made it a hit with young boys. My favorite Tarzan was Johnny Weissmuller, a former Olympic swimming star who was a master of the Tarzan yell. I liked Maureen O'Sullivan as Jane, and Cheetah as himself. Sometimes all we kids did was hangout and practice our Tarzan yell. If you had a rope to swing on (there weren't many jungle vines in southeast Georgia) and could make this yell, "Aaaaah-ah-ah-ah-aaaah-ah-ah-ah-aaaah," life was good.

Living in rural Georgia as I did with woods and small creeks at every turn, Tarzan movies reminded me of "dangers that lurked in every direction." There were quicksand, snakes, mad dogs and wild cats, praying mantis, scorpions, tarantulas, and lockjaw to be concerned about, or so we thought. Of these, praying mantis and lockjaw worried me the most.

Praying mantises were rare but every kid knew if one spit in your eye you would go blind. This a childhood myth, but every time we saw one, friends volunteered me to kill it. "Allen, you got glasses. It can't spit in your eye."

"Nah," I would reply, "He might spit from the side and go under my glasses."

By the time we got through arguing who was to kill it, the mantis had escaped. Some older kids told us a story about a young boy my age from Davisboro who got spit in the eye and went blind. After that, he couldn't make his own Kool-Aid or peanut butter and jelly sandwiches.

Another childhood misconception was getting lockjaw from stepping on a rusty nail. If you stepped on one and didn't get medical attention right away, your jaw would lock up. Closed, that would be bad. If there were girls around, and there always were with me (my three sisters), any little scratch they got was followed by, "You gonna get lockjaw, you gonna get lockjaw, better tell mama." Silly girls. Some teenage kids told us a story about a boy my age from Oak Park who got lockjaw and had to go to the hospital. His jaw was locked up, closed, and he couldn't eat. At the hospital, they put him on a Kool-Aid-only diet through a straw. That diet wasn't so bad, except he couldn't have any peanut butter and jelly sandwiches.

There was much to be concerned about in the wilds of Georgia during my youth, but I was lucky for I was never blinded by a praying mantis or caught lockjaw. Also, I never saw any scorpions, tarantulas, and apparently worried way too much about quicksand. I got stomach aches several times for eating too many green plums or pears, but those were the only times I ever remember not wanting a cold glass of Kool-Aid and a peanut butter and jelly sandwich.

Runaway Kid

I do not remember why I wanted to run away from home. That memory has been lost over the years. Childlike, I was probably mad about not getting my way, pouting. My parents and sisters would be sad if I left and they realized I was the best kid and brother ever. Too bad, I was gone! That'll show them! I was nine.

The plan was to walk to Bartow, four miles away. The first three miles were a county-maintained dirt road with two wooden bridges, a short bridge over the drainage of a wet weather pond, and a second larger one that spanned Grey Coat Creek. Trees shaded it and made the road tunnel-like with a dark, isolated feel. It was spooky. I had been there once with a friend, but never alone.

The final mile was the heavily traveled US Highway 319, but it was the big bridge that consumed my worries, not the paved road. I knew if Mama had any idea I was about to do such a thing, she would come looking for me. Every adventure, every time I left home exploring the farm, the woods, and beyond, she was adamant to tell me, "Go where you want but don't get on any paved road." (A simple order which I almost always followed.) However, things got seriously complicated when she added," And don't get wet," and "Come home before it gets dark. " It was hard being a curious country boy with all those rules and regulations.

On reaching Bartow I would catch the Nancy Hanks passenger train or a freight one to Atlanta, a three-hour journey. I had cousins there who didn't have sisters and certainly they would understand my plight. For food I packed my favorites: peanut butter and jelly sandwiches and chocolate chip cookies in a brown paper sack, grape Kool-Aid on ice in a quart mason jar. I was traveling light and fast. Goodbye, home.

I snuck out to begin the long journey and quickly made the

crossroads, every bit of two hundred feet from our front porch. I looked both ways (that's what Mama said to do) and kept walking. There on the left was a large pasture with a small pen and watering trough for the cows. Stopping to tell the cows goodbye, the words of leaving choked in my throat, so I mooed instead; it was easier. I would miss them, especially the one called "Old Fool." She always went the wrong way when Dad was moving the herd from one pasture to another. His words directed to her on these occasions were muttered with disgust, "Old Fool."

Next to the cow pen there were five huge water oaks over a hundred years old, parallel to the road and in an evenly spaced row, a cool shady oasis even in the heat of a Georgia summer and one of my favorite places. We played cowboys and Indians under and around those trees. My sisters would be the Indians, and we boys would capture and tie them up. I killed a lot of Indians under those trees. The thought saddened me, but I reckoned they would have Indians in Atlanta, it being a big city and all.

Across the road from the oaks were plum bushes and a blackberry thicket. I figured they might not have those in the city, better have some now. No telling if or when I might get back. A deep ditch and a high clay bank stood in my way, but after several tries, I reached my objective only to be disappointed when I realized it was the wrong time of the year for plums or blackberries. I found some maypops but they are only fun to pop or use for ammo, not to eat. I was hungry, so I sat down in the shade of the fruitless bushes and quickly went through my packed goodies.

Soon back on the road, I plodded this time, dragging my feet. Having eaten all my supplies, I began to have doubts, but the McGowan home (our farm help) was just ahead, and I could stock up. I knew they would have more Kool-Aid as well as cat head biscuits, streak o' lean, (salt pork, for the Yankees) and fried chicken. Mrs. McGowan was a very good cook and always kept extra food on her wood stove. My pal Bobby would be there as well and I needed to say goodbye. Standing in the road just at their house, I turned back to see my home. It seemed far away and small. I had traveled all of five hundred feet.

Bobby met me at the door and I told him I was running away. He was two years older; he smiled. He said come in, have a biscuit. A few minutes later, I heard a tractor out front. It was Dad. He said he needed help thinning the watermelons and after we did that, we could go to town and have a "co-cola" and a moon pie. That sounded much better than running away from home.

I reckoned spooky bridges, busy roads, Bartow, and Atlanta would have to wait. Dad wasn't the kind of fellow you discussed running away with. I still don't know how he knew where I was, but he was smarter and older. It didn't matter. There were many years ahead, with lots of chances to run away. Eventually I did, in a matter of speaking, traveling much farther than Bartow or Atlanta.

Cow Pies

Bobby, my best friend, lived up the road from our house, not more than a hundred yards away. His father was Dad's number one man on the farm. One of our favorite places to hang out was up in the mimosa tree in the side yard. Low branches forked in several places, providing us with an easy climb, comfortable sitting, and a great view of the yard and barns. Sometimes we carried ammo up with us and when my sisters came out, we surprise-attacked them from above. The ammo could be magnolia bulbs, maypops, or even rotten eggs, when we were feeling, well, rotten. On this day we had no ammo and were sitting up in the tree talking and considering what our next adventure might be.

We had come up with nothing when Dad came out the backdoor and spied us sitting in the mimosa. He said, "You boys want to make some money?"

The answer was easy, "Yes, Sir!"

He went on, "OK, go clean out the barn behind the tool shed and lay down fresh oat straw. There we will spread out the soon-to-be harvested new potatoes."

We figured this would be an easy job and we were right. We knew those barns well and at any one time knew what was in them. This one had some old straw from the previous year's potato crop, two partially filled sacks of moldy corn seed, and a few rusty plow points.

We went to work and talked of how we would spend our imminent windfall. Pay was likely to be a quarter each for two or three hours of work, pretty good money for boys in those times. An educated guess would make it a couple dollars in today's money. For sure, we could buy a coke and some candy, making this Saturday a good one. The only problem was getting to the store.

Getting a parent to drive you the store to buy cokes and candy was hard, if not impossible. They considered it a waste of gas and time. Each of the two stores available was only a mile away, so we figured as soon as we finished and got paid, we would walk. We went about our work. As we were finishing, dad came over, inspected, pronounced it a good job, and, "sure as shootin," gave us each a quarter.

I took off for the house and told mama we were going to go to the store. She said, "You boys mind yourselves and don't get on the highway."

The highway was the US # 1 and, at that time, one of the busiest in America. We left the house feeling good. Spider, the family dog, tagged along. Every now and then I would reach in my pocket and feel the quarter. Along the way there was discussion of possible purchases with the excitement only the young can muster.

A hundred yards or so from our destination we had a decision to make, for it was mama's rule that we stay off the highway. We could go left across an open field and come out behind Meadow-Brett's store, the easy way, or we could go right, climb over a fence, walk through a pasture with eyes out for the bull and the cows, climb over another fence, cross the railroad tracks, and come out behind Mr. Jimmy's store.

We chose to go the hard way, partly because we liked Mr. Jimmy, a kindly old man, and partly because we wanted to see Spider eat some cow pies. Bobby and I found this habit of Spider's to be funny, even funnier when we got back home and my sisters would kiss our cow-pie-eating dog right on the mouth. We climbed over the barbed fence; Spider squirmed under it and went about his nasty habit.

I interrupt the telling of this tale to inform city slickers and those that know little of bovines that cow pies are defined by Merriam-Webster as "a dropping of cow dung." I might also add similarly shaped as a homemade pie. Please feel free to Google it if further clarification is needed.

We soon got to the store. I have made some hard decisions in my life, but I don't believe many of them have been much harder than how best to spend a quarter at a country store in the late fifties. We could buy a drink and a candy bar easily with a quarter. The difficulty was in choosing a preferred drink with Coke's, RC's, and Nehi's cooling in Mr. Jimmy's ice box. Then it was a near impossible decision with the candy: Baby Ruth, Zero, Butterfinger, Three Musketeer, not to mention jars full of penny candy. Often, after finishing the treats, I regretted my choices and it felt like a loss.

Today a poor choice of candy or drink bothers me a lot less than it did during my youth: I have grown up. But sadly, I no longer have a cow-pie-eating dog as a companion and friend and that is truly a loss.

Doc

There was a time when you could find one in every small town, the family doctor. To the townspeople they were usually called "Doc." They doctored dad, mom, and the children, grandpa, grandma, your aunts, uncles, and cousins. These small-town doctors knew the family history, medical and otherwise. Our town had the best doctor I have ever known.

I met him on the first day of my life in 1949. My life began in his clinic, supposedly the first boy child born there. Two girls preceded me. He brought me into this world and got it started proper with a spank right where young boys need it the most. I would need more as I grew, but those were not in his job description. Dad provided those. "Doc" doctored me through just about every childhood ailment known, including but not limited to measles, mumps, chicken pox, flu, colds, and chiggers. I was most appreciative of the help with the chiggers. (Frequent scratching does not describe the ailment adequately.) Until I was nearly thirty, he was just about the only doctor I ever saw.

I don't remember him calling me anything but Goodson, my last name. Maybe that was his manner, I am not sure. Whatever the reason, I didn't mind. As I grew up, I learned to appreciate his manner and common-sense approach to my well-being. There was a time in my twenties when I felt run down with no energy. Twenty-something folks shouldn't feel like that, so I went to see the him. He asked a few questions, did a short physical exam and said, "Go over to White Kitchen's grocery store and get the biggest T-Bone steak they got. You will be fine." He was right. Best prescription I ever received!

When I turned thirteen, I got a social security card and my first paying job other than working on the farm. I was hired by a local grocery to deliver sales papers to every house in town. It paid better than farm work and was easier. Unfortunately, my delivery career was short lived. On the very first day I was hit by a car while making the rounds on my bicycle. It wasn't the driver's fault; I violated the cardinal rule of cycling, look before crossing the street. I can tell you from very personal experience, if a car hits a bicyclist at thirty-five miles per hour, the car wins.

I can also tell you, if you elect to get run over, do it in front of the doctor's house. Yes, I had just delivered his sales paper and was crossing the street to deliver one to the Methodist preacher's house when I got hit. As if planned, I had my medical needs covered on one side of the street and I had my spiritual needs covered on the other. Fortunately for me, the undertaker who lived three blocks away wasn't needed.

Doc told me later he had been standing at the window, saw the whole thing, grabbed his bag, and came running. If I live to be a hundred and sixty-five, I will never forget the sight of him and mama looking down at me when I regained my consciousness lying there on the sidewalk.

I got banged up and spent a week in the hospital with a concussion. For the next year I went for monthly EEG's (or spelled out, electroencephalogram.) In the end I was declared healthy. It might have been worse without the best doctor I have ever known being Johnny-on-the-spot. My three sisters, none of whom ever went to medical school, claim I was never right after that. They might be onto something.

Lawrence Welk and Liver

Growing up in the fifties and early sixties, we had two TV stations: Channel 6 and Channel 12, both sixty miles away in Augusta, GA. We watched on a twenty-three-inch Motorola TV, a large size for the times. In the early sixties the first color shows begin to appear, but our TV was black and white only. Some times when the weather was extra cloudy, someone had to go outside and turn the antenna to get good reception; otherwise, Beaver, Wally, and Eddie would be "snowed" out, leaving me with Lawrence Welk to watch. I'd rather eat liver.

Being the only boy, I was the one to go out and turn the antenna. It was atop a pipe that ran from the ground to above the roof of our home. This task often turned into a circus. One of my sisters would stand by the window, watch the TV, and yell instructions to me. "OK, turn it Allen, some more, turn some more, some more, wait that's it, no, no, you went too far. Turn it back, some more, some more, little more. OK, that's it. Wait, what did you just do, Allen?"

"Nothing, I let go of the pipe."

"Well, put your hands on the pipe. That's it, stay right there."

"Are you crazy? I can't stay out here and hold the pipe; it's twenty-five degrees."

Just what I wanted, another Lawrence Welk and his champagne music Saturday night. I'd rather eat liver.

In all honesty, I would sneak a few peeks if the Lennon Sisters were on just to see Kathy, the hottest of the Lennon Sisters. I had a crush on her. But that was all I could take and would find something else to do. (For you younger readers, the Lennon Sisters were not John Lennon's grandma, aunts, or related in any way, but a totally different clan, especially with their music.)

When Lawrence Welk was the only show available to watch, I would go to my sisters' room. They had a record player. Unfortunately for me, my older sister Patsy was an Elvis groupie and she was playing Elvis. She once played "Love Me Tender" 745 times in a row. I'd rather eat liver.

On a side note when my sisters got their first record player, the electricity bill went up sixty-five cents for the month. Dad hit the roof. He wasn't a hard man, but he just hadn't figured record playing in his budget. Besides he was a small farmer trying to feed and clothe a family and there wasn't much extra money to go around. One of my sisters suggested the power company had gotten it wrong, but Dad knew that wasn't so. In those days the power company sent customers a postcard with dials on it that matched the meter outside. You took a pencil and drew the clock-like arms on the dials and send it back. They then figured your bill and sent it out. Try that system today. I believe folks were honest in those times, but I can imagine some fellow in a foul mood because of being served liver for supper, deciding to take it out on the power company and drawing those clock arms on the postcard to his advantage. This may well have been true, for it wasn't long after the power company started sending a man around to read the meters.

Anyway, finding nothing else to do, I went back to the living room and checked in on Mom, Dad, and Lawrence. Myron Floren, the accordion player, and Joe Feeny, the singer, were bringing down the house with a duet. I grabbed a jacket, went outside, and sat on the porch with the dog, twenty-five degrees or not. He could sing better than Joe Feeny; he was good company, and he always ate my liver. I sure miss that dog.

❦ 3 ❦

Growing Up

My Sisters Patsy and Judy

Birds and Bees

I have always been somewhat confused about things, especially so when it comes to "the birds and the bees" and females. Growing up on a farm with animals all around, I had a head start on most. I witnessed first-hand amore between boy and girl cows. On one of the first such viewings, I asked dad, "What are they doing?"

He replied, "Playing."

With such an answer, I guess he figured me too young for the birds and bees talk. Certainly, his answer didn't help much, for it was unlike any play I knew about. Later I learned from the older boys that they were making babies, an answer I cared about even less. "Playing" seemed like much more fun. Later in life I would learn about courtship between humans, but I never saw that between farm animals. A moo here, a moo there, and favors were won. It turned out not to be so easy in the human world.

Since dad was very little help, TV played a role in my early birds and bees education, but even that was confusing. Most of my cowboy heroes didn't bother with girls; they were too busy fighting Indians or herding cows and were apparently in the dark as much as I was about the cow thing. Roy Rogers had Dale, prettiest cowgirl I knew at the time, but he seemed to favor Trigger more. I was fine with that. Marshall Dillon had Miss Kitty, but their relationship seemed strictly platonic. I think the only reason the Marshall hung out with her was because she owned a saloon and beer was on the cheap. Another TV hero was Tarzan. Tarzan had Jane; she was pretty and wore skimpy clothes to boot. I saw Tarzan kiss Cheetah, but never once did he kiss Jane. I was a shy, confused country boy, but that wouldn't have been my choice.

Up until age ten or so, I didn't like girls much. Around eleven or twelve, I was getting over that. I was still confused, but I was much more willing to learn all there was to know. As it happened about this time in my life, one night at the county fair I won a teddy bear. The perfect make-points-with-a-girl gift I thought. There was a girl in my class at school, a long-haired brunette, willowy type who had caught my eye. She was smart and knew all about the Beatles. Better yet, we rode the same school bus every day.

I fantasized in my mind the night before how it would go. I would get on the bus with the teddy bear, walk down the aisle to my new sweetie, smile, and place the teddy bear gently in her lap. She would be so overcome with love, lust, and I don't know what all, that I would grab her up in my arms and kiss her dead away on the lips, just like I had seen Tarzan kiss Cheetah. OK, that's a poor example, but that was about the extent of kissing I had seen. Young love doesn't always work out quite the way you plan it and neither did it this time. I got on the bus, my legs shaking so badly I could hardly walk, my mouth so dry I could neither talk nor pucker. I threw the thing at her and ran to the back of the bus. Laughter broke out. I was humiliated. I had a lot to learn.

Some fifty odd years since that memorable day, I am much more comfortable in the company of a fair maiden; my legs rarely get shaky, and my pucker is just fine. I still have a lot to learn though. The best way to sum up the man I am today is with the line I read somewhere, "I am too old to be dangerous and still young enough not to realize it." I have, however, learned that a female's heartfelt smile, be she two or ninety-two is one of life's simplest and best pleasures.

Some say this "birds and bees" thing is what makes the world go round. You will get no argument from this old Georgia farm boy.

Nekkid Statue

The Nancy Hanks changed my world. I was nine when I made my first trip to Atlanta, which I knew was the state capitol and a big city, but that was about it. A trip was planned for a couple cousins and me to visit relatives. We would ride the Nancy Hanks to Atlanta, and they would pick us up at the station. If you don't know about the Nancy Hanks, you must not be from around these parts. If you are from these parts and don't know about the Nancy Hanks, you will be required to turn in your Southern papers at the end of this story.

The Nancy Hanks was a magnificent blue and grey painted passenger train that made the trip from Savannah to Atlanta and back, every day. It was named for a famous race horse who had been named for Abraham Lincoln's mother. Sort of ironic, since Abe, while respected, wasn't particularly cared for in the Deep South. Abe had picked the wrong side during the War of Northern Aggression.

I had seen the Nancy Hanks often but had never been onboard. We laid pennies on the track ahead of its arrival in town and after it passed were instant owners of smashed flat ones. One of the rich kids did this with a nickel. It was shiny and impressive after being squashed. I would have liked having the same, but a nickel at the time bought either a coke or full-sized candy bar. Money was hard to come by for this farm boy, and so I admired his flat nickel and spent my few found five cent pieces on gastric pleasures.

On this day, we boarded the train with money in our pockets, bagged lunches, and wide eyes. The ride was exciting and entertaining for a country boy whose longest trip up to now was sixty miles by car to Augusta for school clothes. At times the Nancy's speed was impressive, at other times slow. There were huge trestles when we crossed rivers and creeks. We went through small towns and large ones. Folks stood by the tracks all along the way and waved. We waved back. It was the fifties and waving to strangers was something you did.

Picking us up at the train station, our cousins drove us to their home in their air-conditioned car. In fact, their whole house was air conditioned. There were no gnats, not one. All this was way more comfortable than the world I grew up in. I was afraid to touch anything. They had a walk-in basement with a concrete floor, first one I had ever seen. Our country farm home had a three-foot crawl space a boy could play in and find doodle bugs, but I couldn't stand up and had knots on my head to prove it. I immediately planned to ask Dad to build us one when we got home. They lived on what we country boys called a dead-end road; in Atlanta they called it a cul-de-sac. I had a lot to learn.

The relatives toured us all around the city and even a few miles out of town to the biggest rock I had ever seen. Back down on the farm it was hard to find a good size rock for my slingshot. (I mostly ended up using chinaberries.) Stone Mountain it was called. Some one claimed there was much more underground. We hiked a mile up one side to the top, where we could see far away, including tall buildings of downtown Atlanta. Carved on one side and bigger than life were Robert E. Lee, Stonewall Jackson, and Jefferson Davis on their horses, Southern heroes from the War of Northern Aggression.

The next day we went to the airport, a place that is more than a little trouble to visit in today's world, but in the late fifties, you could walk in like you owned the place. An observation deck was there for sightseers. We stood in awe of huge, shiny planes landing and taking off every few minutes. Fixed coined-operated telescopes allowed for closer viewing. Having never seen a passenger plane other than on TV, I would have spent my last nickel doing just that if we hadn't run out of time.

On our last day, we visited a famous department store called Rich's. We rode an elevator to the top; outside on the roof was this huge statue of a man seventeen feet tall. They said his name was David, a famous king from the Bible, they said. They said the statue had been brought all the way from Italy as an exhibit and was touring America. I didn't know what to make of it because it was a man in his birthday suit, "nekkid" as the day he was born. All his parts were showing, right there on top of Rich's in broad daylight and in front of everyone. It's art, my relatives explained. I was embarrassed. Back home on the farm, I had seen similar "nekkidness" with farm animals, but we never put one on the front porch and invited the neighbors over to view it.

That is the story of my first trip to Atlanta, it was not to be my last one. The Nancy Hanks took me there and brought me home several more times. She was a big part of my youth and almost the same age. She was born in 1947; I was born in 1949. She retired in 1971 when I was twenty-one. My adult life was just starting. By most standards of the day I was supposed to be an adult or at least getting there. Some would say I was making a poor job of it. They had a point. I was a country boy and I had a lot to learn.

Giddy up!

My equine experience began at a young age. I couldn't have been more than eleven. Neighbors offered us ponies to enjoy as long as we kept them well fed and in good health. Trigger and Diablo were their names. We kept them in good health, but they came close to ruining mine.

When I learned what Diablo meant in English, it gave me pause. I didn't know Spanish at the time, but it also must have meant, "Stand on boy's foot" for he did that, frequently. No amount of pushing would get him off my foot. He moved when he was ready. I overlooked this in the beginning, figuring a ride that didn't require pedalling was a much better way to get around. That was my first mistake with these two nags.

My second mistake was trying to feed Trigger an apple. Either he didn't care or didn't know the difference between apples and thumbs. Only due to my cowboy-like reflexes do I have all ten digits today. If feeding him an apple was a danger, there was no way was I going to offer a small lump of sugar. He might have been named after Roy Roger's horse, but he didn't act the part at all.

After a time, we began riding both horses bareback because keeping a saddle on them became impossible. Bridle them up and they would be fine for a few minutes. Then for some reason known only to them and God, they would take off running as fast as they could go. Did you know that ponies can stop on a dime? They can, and they did. When that happens, momentum takes over. Momentum goes like this: Pony is running fast as he can and suddenly stops on a dime; boy has momentum and keeps going forward. Mama told me often I was a hard head, so I tried to land on mine. She was right about that since I never got hurt once.

I also learned a pony can make a ninety degree turn at full speed. Momentum works the same way, except the horseless rider is flung off the side, while the pony continues on his way. Only my cowboy-like landings saved me from sure damage to my well-being. A person can break his neck doing a thing like that.

There were times I wanted to punch Trigger between the eyes with my fist, but I thought this must be against cowboy rules. I was reminded of what my parents had said to me several times, "This will hurt me more than it hurts you." Punching a pony might be the same thing. I could break my fist doing a thing like that.

We rode those ponies for a summer and decided that life was too short to die or be made lame as cowboys. Dad agreed and took both back to the neighbors who owned them. I reckoned I wasn't cut out to be a cowboy; besides, as was seen on TV, all cowboys had for supper was beans and coffee. Who wants that?

What is That?

Pointing at the serving, I asked my classmate Arthur a time-honored question about mystery meat served in school lunches. "What is that?" He replied with his mouth full and chewing on the aforementioned dish, "I don't know, but it's good." Arthur wasn't the most reliable critic; he was a growing boy with a huge appetite. He ate everything. I poked it with my fork, hesitating to taste it. The American actress Hattie McDaniel in the greatest movie ever made, *Gone with the Wind*, summed up some of our lunches, "It ain't fittin, it just ain't fittin."

Times certainly have changed since the fifties and sixties, as have schools and school lunches. We called it the "lunch room," for it was the only meal served there. Today they are called cafeterias. Cafeterias generally serve a variety of foods to allow for choice but there was no choice for us. We began by grabbing a tray, a plastic glass for milk, silverware, and went down the line. Handed to us at the end of the line was a compartmental plate with one meat, two vegetables, bread, and small dessert. The challenge was figuring out what you had just been served. Like it or not.

There weren't many complaints from parents about the cost. One dollar got each student a meal ticket for the entire week, five lunches at twenty cents each. The price rose to a dollar and a quarter before I graduated, but still by all measures a good value. My complaint, as it was with most of my friends, (mystery meat aside) was the vegetables served. There were entirely too many days with cooked carrots, lima beans, rutabagas, and the ever-unpopular English pea, (commonly called by us growing scholars as china berries.) Also, there were white lima beans, dry and different tasting from the green butter beans we grew on the farm and were used to. I heard a person call them Northern beans and it should have been against the law to serve food in the deep South called Northern anything.

If this occurred in today's world, students might file a Class Action lawsuit, but this was way back when and Class Action lawsuits hadn't yet been invented. Students complained but the complaints fell on deaf ears. Like it or not.

Today adults are concerned about overweight kids. This wasn't a problem when I went to school. Active recess and uneatable lunches took care of that. I can imagine some school administrator high up the chain saying, "Fat kids? Feed them Northern beans, rutabagas, and china berries. They won't eat them; problem solved."

To be honest, I must tell you that things improved in my eighth year of school. We got a new principal, a burly man, and just by looking at him you knew he enjoyed food. He also happened to be a very good math teacher. He taught me Algebra II, Geometry, and Trigonometry. It's not that he changed the everyday menus; what he did was add more - all the homemade biscuits and syrup we wanted with an unlimited supply of cold milk to wash them down. When we were knee-deep in china berries, rutabagas, Northern beans, and the mystery meat was too much of a mystery, we boys could fill up on biscuits and milk. It's a fact that Southern boys can live on biscuits alone.

Today, schools with vending machines offer soft drinks, crackers, chips, and candy bars as options for a disappointing lunch. There were no vending machines in our day. Junk food, as it is called, was not to be had, but at the door of the lunchroom stood a freezer with ice cream treats. With a dime, we could buy a popsicle, fudgesicle, drumstick, or a Betty, known today as an ice cream sandwich. If I had two dimes, I would buy myself and the delightful, dark-haired, curvaceous Marilyn Beacham and love of my life a treat. If I had only one dime, I would buy a popsicle, break it into halves, keep one half for myself and give the other to Marilyn. Sharing a popsicle meant we were a couple, but Marilyn wouldn't fall for the idea. According to her, at times I was immature and therefore not worthy of her affection. Ah, those wonderful years of innocence, when true love and tasty school lunches were hard to come by.

Lessons of My Youth

There was this particular time in my youth that I wanted a new bicycle. Actually, there were a lot of times I wanted a new bike. (Wanting is a disease of the youth and I had a double dose.) The bicycle I had at the time was cobbled together from two older ones. It was ragged, rusty, and with neither a chain guard or fenders, a pitiful looking thing. I had seen a new one at Parker Hardware store in downtown Wadley, a magnificent red Western Flyer with lots of shiny chrome. It had a kickstand, a horn, and all the things of a young boy's dreams. The price was $19.95, a large sum of money for a farm boy in 1959. It was an especially large amount since I didn't have any. None. Zero. Zilch. $19.95 plus tax was what I needed.

So, I set about trying to figure how I could get this bike. Christmas and my birthday were months away. I couldn't wait that long; a few months to a ten-year-old is like, "FOREVER!" I needed it now. I could ask Dad to buy it for me, but I knew in advance what he would say. "I don't have any money for a bicycle, but you can work and save up." I had heard this before. He was a broken record when it came to my needs and he was big on "work and save up." He was teaching me a lesson. I didn't want any lesson. I wanted a shiny new Western Flyer bicycle, the red one from Parker Hardware store.

After his expected reply, I looked for ways to make money around the farm. As it turned out, it was cotton picking season. Dad always had ten to twenty acres planted and hired folks to pick the harvest ready cotton. School was in so I only had Saturday to pick. Being young and inexperienced in the ways of the financial world, I assumed that I would be able to buy that bike after just one day of picking cotton. I was soon to learn differently. There are hard lessons a ten-year-old boy has to learn. I didn't care much for that part of life as a young boy. Frankly, I don't much care for it at sixty-eight but have learned to handle it some better.

Saturday morning, I was up at dawn, packed a lunch of peanut butter and jelly sandwiches, cookies, and a quart jar of iced Kool-Aid. Dad loaded up all the pickers in his truck and drove us down to the cotton field. We were given a sack with a strap to pick with and a flat burlap sheet to dump our sacks of cotton on. Easy enough. Truth is, I worked as hard as possible on this day, from dawn to dusk. I picked cotton and dumped each full sack on the sheet. It was a big pile at the end of the day, but not nearly as large as the grown folks. Dad and Mr. Albert came around, weighed the picker's cotton, and paid each worker on the spot. I could hardly wait. They hooked the scales to mine, lifted it up, Dad looked at the scales and said, "Ninety-seven pounds, good job." The pay was three cents a pound, two dollars and ninety-one cents total. I have never been more disappointed in my life. I was old enough to do math. Six more Saturdays. "Work and save up" was not my idea of fun, and I certainly didn't have the patience for it.

All the pickers loaded in the truck and Dad drove us home. I was tired and disappointed. The first thing I saw as we pulled up in the yard was my old bicycle leaning against the house. It didn't have a kickstand nor was it shiny like the new ones, but I could ride it without picking any cotton. Then I remembered, Christmas is only three months away. Santa might bring me a new one.

Almost miraculously, cotton picking at three cents a pound that day had bought me a little patience.

Bovine Adventures

My father was a cow man. Each year after corn was harvested for silage, he would travel to the foothills of the Smoky Mountains, specifically to Statesville, North Carolina, which was about two hundred and seventy-five miles. There he would buy calves in lots of one hundred to fatten up for the market. Interstates did not exist, so he and the cows had to maneuver through dozens of small southern towns that were particularly proud of their single red light. This long trip "upset" the calves something terrible. More on that later.

Dad, usually gone a couple of nights, came home ahead of the calves and brought with him gifts for us four children and mama. For himself he also brought a mason jar full of what they called apple brandy. They lied. It was apple moonshine. One day, being the inquisitive types, my pal Bobby and I decided we needed to try it. I went first and nervously took a small swallow. It burned my lips, mouth, tongue, throat, and everything it passed on the way to my stomach. As soon as I could breathe again and my eyes quit watering, all I could get out was "good." I lied. Since Bobby was older and tougher than I, he took a bigger swallow. He stopped breathing, and his eyes watered. He recovered faster and said, "Good stuff." He lied.

(Sorry, I got sidetracked, back to the calves.) They always arrived in the dead of the night, loaded on a double decker trailer pulled by a semi. There was a sense of urgency to get them unloaded, get water and feed in them, and settled down. Take note of the following fact because it will help you visualize the last part of this story: Cows have four stomachs.

My job was at the end of the trailer to keep the calves moving and to adjust the chute when we emptied the lower deck and began with the upper deck. Dad and the other men would keep the calves moving down the chute and into the paddock. When it came time to start with the upper deck, I found myself on the wrong side. I needed to either go all the way around the front of the semi or take a shortcut under the trailer. I chose the shortcut.

As luck would have it, just as I was exiting to the other side of the trailer, one of those lovely red coated calves decided to unload the entire contents of her four upset stomachs on yours truly. Either due to my youthful wisdom or just an ordinary slip of the tongue, I was able to sum up both the material on me as well as my current feelings about the situation with one four letter word, "sh*t!"

Up to this point in my young life, I had never uttered a four-letter word in front of my Dad and he had never uttered one in front of me. What little I knew about profanity at that time I had heard from older boys. I looked up to see his reaction. On his face was the sly grin he carried for life and he said to me, "It will wash off." He was right, that kind will wash off. Other kinds not so much.

4

Perspective

Mama

Boys will be Boys

It was Friday and June and South Georgia hot. A campout with three of my friends from town was the plan. We packed hot dogs, sardines, Vienna sausages, saltines, cookies, and co-colas -- a feast, or at least our thirteen-year-old stomachs thought so. Loaded with an ample supply of provisions and sleeping bags, we headed to a wooded site a mile away. Far from watchful eyes, we set up camp, built a fire, and soon a number of inevitable teenage dares began. We were young and foolish, and we were going to get in trouble because we were just that.

I could name the individual who suggested what we were about to do, but in the last fifty-odd years he has lived a Christian life and has corrected his ways. Besides, we were in it together and were all to blame. The aim was to push over an outhouse, a deed considered in that time and place a coming of age thing, like a first kiss only different. As it turned out, I enjoyed my first kiss considerably more. We knew the exact location of a neatly kept "two holer" close by. With target in mind and using the woods for cover, we reached our objective quickly. And though there was other mischief that night, it was the stealthy attack on the outhouse that got me nabbed by the authorities.

The next morning, just after my cohorts had gone home, the Sheriff and his deputy drove up in our yard. He knew everybody in the county and everyone knew him. Fortunately for me, he was a fair man. They got out of the car, the deputy tall and skinny, the Sheriff heavy-set, dressed in a suit and ready for business. With authority in his words, he asked,

"Allen, were you boys messing around last night?"

I stammered around with some "no sir's" and "yes sir's" but never really confessed to anything,

After listening to my rambling, he says, "Where's your Daddy?"

I mumbled, "He's in the watermelon patch."

He says, "Get in and we'll go see him. The folks might want to press charges."

The deputy put me in the back of the cruiser and slammed the doors shut. Door handles had been removed on the inside; there was no escape. I saw empty co-cola cans, a chocolate chip cookie package, and a hot dog bun wrapper on the floorboard: evidence. This wasn't looking good.

The watermelon patch was over a mile away and during the ride wild thoughts were going through my head. Among other things, I tried to remember if the hanging judge was still in office. When we pulled up, Dad was in the middle of the watermelon patch sweating bullets on a miserable one hundred degree, dead-still Southern summer day. Seeing us approach, he stopped working, took off his hat, wiped the sweat from his brow, and watched the Sheriff and me coming across the field. I was scared to death. I do not, under any circumstance, recommend troubling your father while he is working watermelons on a hot Saturday afternoon, especially with matters involving the authorities. Few men of the time had patience for a young boy's foolishness, certainly not my Father. After a handshake, couple of "how you doing's," and a "hot enough for ya," the sheriff got down to business. "Emmett, looks like the boys were clowning around last night and pushed over Washington's outhouse. He might want to prosecute." My father stared at me with a look I had never seen. If his stare had of been X-Ray vision, he would have burned a hole clean through me.

Fortunately, the man whose outhouse we had turned over (he called it his laboratory) was kind, gracious, and forgiving. Standing before him, busted for the crime, and unable to look him in the eye, I heard Mr. Washington say these words, "I don't reckon those boys meant any harm. It's all right."

This good man and the High Sheriff let me off the hook. Dad wasn't as forgiving and sentenced me to life without parole. Eventually, he went soft, as he always did, and I earned a pardon by working my tail off in the watermelon patch without pay during the hottest June and July on record.

Of the many experiences in a sixty-year life, a few are unforgettable memories, particularly those of your own making. This one is remembered for the forgiveness of a kind man with an outhouse, the High Sheriff, and my dad. They were grown men, but I am sure they remembered from their youth that boys will be boys.

On Sunday

Other than the café, nothing was open. There was no work, no shopping, no ball games. Few cars were out on the road. The town was quiet all day. These were the Sundays of my youth.

In my home town the Baptist and Methodist churches were built back to back with adjoining parking lots. We were Baptist, and it was a common occurrence at the end of the service to come out and find the Methodists long gone. Southern Baptist preachers were long winded and still are, it seems. I'm not sure why. Maybe we have more stubborn sinners.

After church it was straight home for Sunday dinner, yes dinner. That's what Southerners called the midday meal. Yankees called it something else; they are wrong. On Sundays it was fried chicken or pot roast, served with three or four vegetables, dessert, and pitchers of sweet iced tea. After dinner and some rest, we loaded in the car to visit Grandma. My sisters always got shotgun, a seat by the window.

"They are girls, Allen. Let them have it," I heard all too often when I complained. Shotgun was prized, for the view year-round and for the cool breeze coming through the window in summer. Few cars had air conditioning and ours certainly didn't.

First visit was to Grandma Goodson, who lived on the home place in the country. My uncle and his family, which included cousins my age, would be there as well. There was always some kind of refreshments. The adults usually sat on the porch talking, weather permitting, while we kids explored the farm and barns. Two memories stick with me: first, her drive was paved with concrete strips, just the tire ruts. I thought this was very cool and a fancy addition to any home. Secondly, there was a pear orchard. Too many green pears will give you a stomach ache, a lesson I never seemed to learn.

Next was a visit to Big Mama, my maternal grandmother. She lived in town. There were five daughters, three lived in Millen, one in Vidalia, and, of course, my mom in Wadley. They visited but distance made it harder and less frequent for them. Big Mama would have a small Coke and a piece of homemade cake or pie for each of us. Again, adults sat on the porch and talked, kids played in the yard. I once caught a mouse in her shrubbery and gave it to my younger sister. The mouse bit her hand and Big Mama freaked out. After large quantities of hydrogen peroxide, and I don't know what all, Big Mama calmed down. My sister lived. I would have given the mouse to the older two sisters as well, but by this time they were both boy crazy and no longer played with me.

Our visiting done, we went home for supper. My mama took Sunday evenings off from cooking and we kids were left to fend for ourselves. For my meal I searched for desserts; banana pudding or coconut pie were preferences, still are all these years later. When none were found, I complained. "Mama, there is nothing to eat and I am starving to death."

She would brush these remarks aside and suggest things I hated like the leftover liver from Saturday night supper. It took all the Baptist learning in me as well as Mom's enduring threat, "You better straighten up and fly right," to answer in a socially polite way. Our self-served meal completed, we got ready for Baptist Training Union, called BTU, and the evening worship service. Sometimes after church we were invited to Mr. Cloud's. He was the local TV repairman and had a color TV, the first one in town. We watched "Bonanza" in color. I liked Hoss; my sisters liked Little Joe. I mentioned the boy-crazy thing earlier.

Sundays might sound busy. They weren't. The town was closed, nothing but church and visiting grandmas, slow and easy. They were the Sundays of my youth.

A Fair to Remember

They came to town in the fall of the year, their appearance apparently timed with the farm harvest when money was a little more plentiful. The best of times was in the fall after the cotton was picked and the corn harvested. My friends and I never knew the date in advance but prayed for its arrival. We knew for sure when their signs appeared, big black, white, and yellow cardboard signs nailed to telephone poles with handwritten script announcing the dates. The Fair is coming!

A fair was the biggest thing to come to our town. There wasn't much to get excited about in a small Georgia town, but the fair was a once-a-year experience that appealed to all our five senses at the same time. Barking carnies, thrilling rides, colorful lights and tents, smells of cotton candy, and saw dust – all brought excitement to our conservative rural community.

Arriving early in the week, the fair set up quickly, stayed for the week, and left late Saturday night or early Sunday morning after emptying the pockets of every young boy and some of the men. Money was hard to come by anytime, and the week after the fair it was nearly impossible.

The first one I remember set up across the railroad tracks on a two-acre vacant lot. It wasn't the largest of fairs, but there was a Ferris wheel, swings, a tilt-a-whirl, a scrambler, a rock-o-plane, and a small roller coaster. All were relatively safe with the exception of the scrambler, which was fine as long as you took the correct seating position. Choose the outside position and you would be pounded into submission by friends flung against you as this thing spun around and around, faster and faster.

There would be a sideshow with a two-headed calf, a bearded lady, a fire eater, and a sword swallower. The fire eater and sword swallower were the same guy, a rough looking character you wouldn't want to meet in a dark alley. We never had a "hoochie coochie" show. You would have to go all the way to Augusta to see one of those. I don't know why we didn't have one, but I would venture to guess the proper ladies of town let it be known there would be none of that. It was, after all, the fifties, and these ladies were of "Steel Magnolia" standards. In reality, they wore the pants in the family, although they hadn't yet taken to wearing them in public. That would come years later.

If you had money left after the rides and the sideshows, there were snow cones, cold drinks, cotton candy, peanuts, corn dogs, and candy apples to buy. There were also games of chance. You could toss rings, shoot guns or basketballs, or pick up ducks all the while hoping to win a prize for your sweetie. I won a big teddy bear one year, but I didn't have a sweetie to give it to. There was a girl on my school bus that I liked, although not as much as my dog Spider. Spider had little use for a teddy bear, so I figured I would give it to her hoping for some affection in return, maybe even a kiss. The next morning, I got on the bus, walked down the aisle of the bus shaking like a leaf, and I gave her the teddy bear. She said "Thank you" and nothing else. There were no kisses forthcoming. I was broke from the fair and broken hearted from the rejection of a fair maiden.

Love is hard for a country boy, but young boys rebound quickly. As soon as the talk and stories of the fair began to die down, hope and wishing began for another. We just needed patience to wait for the posted signs, right about cotton picking time. And who knew, I might win another teddy bear, and I might have a new sweetie, and I might get a kiss yet, and it would be a fair to remember.

Water

Water makes up seventy-one percent of the earth's surface, but for young boys it is not enough. My earliest experience with water came from the faucets around our farm home. I took it for granted. My father, on the other hand, recognized it as a precious commodity and costly, from running the well that supplied our home to the potential lack of it for the crops that earned him a living. Because of this awareness, he was adamant about the amount drawn for baths, which limited my play time but provided an excuse when mama sent me back to have another lick at the places on young boys that dirt clings to. Elbows and behind the ears were troublesome spots for me.

As I grew, my youthful fascination with water expanded from a bathtub to mud puddles to branches, to creeks, ponds and rivers. I soon grew to the age when I was permitted with friends to leave the yard and play by the branch fifty yards behind our family home. Mama always reminded me, "Don't come home wet."

At the time, I was not good at following orders, mama's or otherwise, and she was not very forgiving when I came home in that condition.

This branch, often pronounced "brainch" by southern folk, was too small to be considered a creek or stream. It began in the adjacent field as a collection of excessive rain runoff. A dirt road separated the two fields. A small wooden bridge without railings allowed the water to find its way under the road and to continue on through our farm. The bridge was tall and wide enough underneath for young boys to stand freely, get soaked, have imaginary Indian fights, and occasionally stumble upon a water snake, which we steered clear of and let go on his way. This was the early beginnings of my life's policy, "Live and let live." I also learned if one is under a wooden bridge when a vehicle crosses, dirt will fall through the cracks and find its way behind said person's ears. Mama often asked how I got so dirty. There was no way I was gonna tell her I was playing under a flimsy bridge with cars and trucks passing above. Hardheaded yes, stupid no.

After the bridge and during wet weather, the water fanned out to one side where there was a pine thicket. Here I learned the life cycle of frogs, from eggs to tadpoles to young frogs. The land on the other side sloped upward and there dad had built a paddock and loading chute for cattle. Beyond this, the stream gathered depth and speed. On the far side of the field three large sweet gum trees lined one side as it exited our property. Minnows swam here upstream from a pond a quarter of a mile away. In the coldest of winters, it would freeze over and we young Southern boys would attempt, as we had seen on TV, ice hockey. Cold snaps in the South rarely are cold enough to freeze even the shallowest of streams and when they did the ice was thin. We, of course, would end up breaking through and going home cold and wet. Mama got upset when this happened and fussed at me about getting pneumonia. She also sometimes said if I kept this behavior up it would be the death of her. This statement confused me since I was the one who was soaked.

The princesses, my three sisters, rarely went with me to the stream, except for a few times when friends of mine visited. All three were boy crazy. It wasn't a problem though, as they were scared of frogs and any threat to put one in their blouses sent them running home, screaming. "Mama, Mama! Allen is trying to put a frog on me!"

Fortunately, mama wasn't concerned with frogs or a boy's childish threats. They would, however, have been wildly successful with their cries if they had yelled, "Mama, Mama! Allen got wet!"

This branch flowed away from our farm to become the head waters of a pond nearby. That pond overflowed to a stream that fed another pond which spilled into Boggy Gut creek. Boggy Gut drains into Williamson Swamp Creek, which merges with the Ogeechee river east of my home town. The black muddy waters of the Ogeechee, meandering turn after turn, and generally flowing southeast for approximately two hundred miles, eventually empty into the Atlantic Ocean.

I suppose it nearly impossible, but the thought occurs to me that something, a leaf, a twig, maybe a small minnow, something from the small stream behind our house might've made that long journey all the way to the ocean.

I made a similar journey, from branch to ocean, those same years. An aunt and uncle owned a house on St. Simons' Island, GA. Our families began an annual summer vacation, cousins included. The house was white, two stories on a corner lot, with a road of gravel and tar leading to the beach. The street ended abruptly and there was an additional walk through dunes with sand so hot it burned the tough feet of this farm boy. Although it was more than fifty-five years ago, I remember the house, the road and the scorching dunes clearly. I fail to remember my wonder at seeing for the first time the never-ending expanse of water. Perhaps my first thoughts were as they remain today, thoughts captured in the lyrics, ".... still feel small when you stand beside the ocean."

Be it like the small branch I played in as a child or vast like the ocean, water is different from the terra firma we live on – primal maybe and mysterious. I don't know. Perhaps it is like our lives, small and unknowing in the beginning. As years add up, we grow like the waters, fuller and flowing faster.

I count it as a blessing that I can remember the beginning of it all, me and that small branch. It seems as close to my youth as I can get.

Black Eyed Peas

I woke just as the sun was coming up. It was a Saturday morning, the only mornings I had much enthusiasm for. Monday through Friday were school days and Sunday was church. School was bad enough, but going to Sunday School for an hour, and then having to sit still on a hard-wooden pew and behave myself while a Baptist preacher went on and on during the Sunday service was near torture. I don't know how he knew I coveted Billy Watson's Lionel train, or just plain coveted Marilyn Beacham. I was thirteen and leaving the years of innocence; Marilyn was the same age and getting curvy.

The night before Dad had asked me a question about work (which I didn't care for, but working for my father meant money, which I always cared for.) We had been sitting on the front porch after supper when he stood to go to bed, turned to me, and said, "You want to plant some black-eyed peas tomorrow?" There were only two answers to this question, "Yes sir" or "No sir." If I said "No sir," he would be fine with that and would get it done without me. "No sir" would also keep me broke, so I said, "Yes sir." I figured if I had money, I could walk down to Mr. Jimmy Steven's store later Saturday afternoon and buy a Yoo Hoo chocolate drink and a honey bun. I figured further if I had money left over, I could also buy my new honey bun Marilyn something, too.

On work mornings I was to be at the barn just after the sun came up. I crawled out of bed, washed my face, brushed my teeth, put on some work clothes, and ate a bowl of Rice Krispies. Quickly out the back door, I was greeted by Spider, my dog. I rubbed his head as we walked to the barn.

I expected to plant the black-eyed peas the only way I knew how to plant anything, on my knees in the garden with a bag of seeds, but sitting in front of the barn was the tractor with the planter attached. Dad was nowhere to be seen nor was the three-quarter ton farm truck. The grease gun was lying in the door of the barn, and so I reckoned he meant for me to grease the tractor and the planter. He taught me this job couple years earlier mainly because it was a dirty, greasy job. He was big on grease and I had heard him say many times, "Grease and oil are cheaper than parts." As I went about the work, I thought it would be good to have some help and figured Marilyn would make a good helper. Then I remembered I had never seen her dirty except one time in the fifth grade when I hit her with a dodgeball to show my undying love. It didn't end well.

Dad pulled up in the truck as I was finishing my work. He walked over to me and asked, "Got it greased up?"

"Yes sir."

I didn't mention the thing about Marilyn and the dodge ball. He looked at me saying, "I want you to start over by the blueberries and plant eight rows of black-eyed peas. Fill up the planter; the peas are in the croker sack on the truck." I saw the half-filled sack (a burlap bag) just as he had said. "All right, I'm going in the house for a cup of coffee" and walked away.

Now I am here to tell you I had never planted a row of nothing with the tractor. Sure, I had driven it plenty, but planting required an expertise I wasn't sure I had. For one, I had to make nice straight rows; snakey ones were not good. I could go in the house and interrupt Dad's coffee drinking with a lot of questions or I could plant the peas.

I drug the sack of peas out of the truck bed, filled the two seed hoppers, cranked up the tractor, and drove toward the blueberries on the far end of the garden. When I got there, I noticed right away the disc harrow had left a straight furrow alongside of the blueberries. That was convenient. I turned the tractor and put the right wheels dead on the furrow, lowered the planter, shifted to a slower gear, adjusted the throttle, took a breath, and let out the clutch slowly. Holy moly, I was cruising along pretty as you please and following the disc furrow just so. When I got to other side of the garden, I stopped the tractor, started breathing again, and turned back to look at my work. My first two rows ever! You couldn't have pulled a string any straighter. With my confidence building, I turned the tractor and planter around and followed the rows back to the other side, and one more time and then one more time. Eight rows. At thirteen years old, I had created a masterpiece in the family garden. Dad came out just as I finished, surveyed my work, and said, "Nice job, put everything away and let's knock off." He reached in his pocket, pulled out his roll of money, peeled off a five-dollar bill, and handed it to me. "Much obliged." He started to walk away, stopped, turned back toward me, and said, "In a few days they will come up and your pea patch will need hoeing." With that he left and went inside.

Tricky man, my father, I hired out to plant some black-eyed peas and now they were all mine to tend. That included fertilizing, dusting for beetles, and picking. Then I thought, Marilyn might like to help. And I thought again, probably not. She might not have yet gotten over the dodge ball incident.

School Days

In the fall of 1956 I began my formal education. I was six years old, soon to be seven. I was the oldest boy in my class; there was a girl a few days older. Both of us had been held back because we were not the required age to start by December first the previous year. None of this mattered in 1956, although it would be a very big deal some ten years later when I became the first male in the class with a driver's license. (There were a number of other firsts that year, first to have fender bender, first to get pulled over by the cops, and the first to get to second base.)

Wadley Elementary was no more than two miles from our farm. I could have easily walked though I never did. It was southeast Georgia where the land is flat and there was rarely ever snow. If there was, it was gone in a few hours. Walking to school, barefoot, uphill, both ways, in the snow, would be a lie, though I have told that lie or some variation dozens of times.

My three sisters and I rode the short trip to school on a bus. The driver, Mr. Willie, was a kind, soft spoken man. He picked us up every morning the exact same time. How Mother got us all fed and ready I will never know. Being a boy, I was low maintenance, but there were times Mr. Willie had to honk the horn an extra beep or two because one or the other of my sisters hadn't finished with her "big" hair, or makeup, or whatever it is that girls of that age have issues with. I plead ignorance with all that; it's safer that way. My sisters were all boy crazy. I was neither boy nor girl crazy, but on the first day, of my first year of my formal education I was to meet the first ever female to turn my head: Mrs. Jones, the first-grade teacher. It was love at first sight. In today's lingo, she was hot.

The elementary school was built in 1924, the date and dedication carved in a granite corner stone near the front entrance, just in the nick of time for my father and his first year of schooling. He never mentioned falling in love with his first-grade teacher. I hope he did.

The original building housed grades one through five as well as a lunchroom, auditorium, library, principal's office, girls' and boys' bathrooms. A spacious hall ran north and south, left to right, with a wood plank floor worn smooth by hundreds of kids before me. It smelled of sweeping compound, a smell imbedded forever in my olfactory experience. The first grade was on the north end followed by the second, third, and fourth right in order until you reached the South end, interrupted midway by the front entrance, the library, and the Principal's office. The fifth grade was directly across from the fourth. Exits on both ends, the southern one led to the playground. In my six-year-old perspective the hall seemed incredibly large and long. Trying to grasp that journey, and the time it would take, class by class, year after year was unimaginable.

In the exact center of the hall, across from the entrance stood a huge trophy case built of wood and glass, filled with shiny trophies, big and small, trophies awarded in athletics, arts, and scholarly endeavors. Names and years etched in metal confirmed each champion's achievements. At my tender age it seemed impossible I could ever earn such a thing, much less have it placed there for all to see. On each side of the trophy case were wide double doors that opened into the school auditorium.

The auditorium was used for school plays, assemblies, and graduation. I distinctly remember a play with thundering and lightning and was amazed to hear thunder in the room at just the right time. I couldn't for the life of me figure how they did that. It wasn't until later I learned a shake of a large piece of tin emulates the sound.

Once a year a Georgia State Patrol man came by to help us become drivers. I am not sure why we younger kids attended, but likely the teachers needed a break. Who could blame them? He talked and showed movies of the most devastating car crashes imaginable, apparently using a teaching method called, "Scare the Bejesus out of Them." Often, he asked questions, and on one such day he asked two young kids well short of driving age to stand up. To the first boy he asked, "What is the hand signal for a left turn?"

The kid held his left arm straight out.

"Very good," the trooper replied, "You may sit down."

He then asked the next boy, "What is the signal for a right turn?"

The kid held his right arm straight out.

The trooper without missing a beat said, "That would be incorrect; your arm is inside the car and could not be seen by other drivers. You may sit down."

Memories are an odd thing. Some are gone in a blink; others last a lifetime.

By the time I began school, sixth and seventh grade rooms had been added to the original structure near the south end and attached with an open-air covered walk way. The two-story red brick high school sat a short walk away. To a first grader, it might as well have been a hundred miles.

Also, a new modern lunchroom was built, near to the north end. We called it a "lunchroom"; today they say cafeteria. There was one meal served, lunch obviously. A meat, two vegetables, bread, desert, and milk, served on a portion-divided plate. You ate what you got or not at all. We complained.

Seven years I spent in that building, more or less ten percent of the average life, and certainly the most formable years. I have been fortunate that my mother passed on to me her love for the written word; my father, clear thinking and reasoning. These gifts did not immediately translate into learning, for I had my share of struggles. Keeping block letters on the lines of my ABC tablet, cursed cursive writing, multiplication tables, and long division cost me many recesses, but, thanks to the school and the teachers, I learned and grew. At no point since has this foundation failed me.

All these years later the memories are cloudy and blurred, but I haven't forgotten completely those good times: the lifelong friends I made, the teachers, the successes and failures in the classroom, the playground games, and the first love of my life. It's all there. I close my eyes and visualize that hallway that once seemed so long it was unimaginable how I would ever make my way to the end. It didn't take long; it was gone in a flash.

High Cotton

I was born December 23, 1949. Try as I might, I can't remember a thing about the forties, but I can remember the fifties, and in the fifties, cotton was king. I grew up in Georgia, dead center of the "Cotton Belt," which runs from Virginia and all the way through the South to Texas. Every year on our family farm Dad planted ten to twenty acres cotton. That is not much by today's standards but it was plenty enough then, for much of the work was done by hand, so much so that the word "hand" was used to describe a cotton laborer. A person seeing my father with a dozen or so folks in his truck might think, "Those folks must be Mr. Goodson's hands." In the early sixties the mechanized cotton picker came about. I remember the first one I saw. Up until then, I had at times been one of his "hands" in the cotton patch.

I was lucky for a country boy; my father never asked me to work unless I wanted something that cost more than a dollar. Dad had this notion that I would learn a valuable life lesson. "If you earn it, you will appreciate it more." I disagreed, but he was not a "modern" parent and had neither time nor patience for policy discussions with children.

If it was late May or June, when my wants got the best of me, it meant "choppin' cotton." I was young when I chopped my first cotton and was assigned to the older boys who were to supervise me and keep me pointed in the right direction. However, direction wasn't really an issue. You took a row and worked in one direction until you got to the other side of the field, made a U turn and worked your way back. I was so young the first few years that the older boys would work two rows to my one, so we could stay together as we worked across the field.

"Cotton choppin' " is a bit of a misnomer since it's mostly weeds that got chopped, although if the cotton was planted too thick, you took out cotton plants as needed. A hoe was the required tool to do the work and from this came the expression, "He has a long row to hoe." I can tell you from personal experience there is no such thing as a short row in a cotton patch. It's hot work without shade and it's dusty. A day of cotton choppin' was guaranteed to earn a young fella a trip back to a wash tub already full of muddy water to have "another lick at his ears."

I remember clearly a twelve-acre field of cotton behind our farm home that produced an incredible three bales per acre. A record-breaking yield for the time, but try as I might, I can't recall the heat. Today at my advanced age the heat feels unbearable. Somehow, we tolerated it in those youthful times. I do remember that the shade of a tree and a quart mason jar filled with ice water was next to heaven on earth. My best friend Bobby said at the time it was hotter than forty hells. He was eleven and knew a lot more than I did at nine. The only hell I knew was the one the Baptist preacher spoke of on Sunday. He made it sound nasty and a place no one wanted to visit. I felt the same way about the cotton patch. I wondered if the preacher had been a farm boy.

I picked cotton later in the year when the crop was ready and my wants again got ahead of my funds. As a kid I was always wanting and always broke. Inflation had kept pace and things I wanted still cost more than a dollar. Hot, backbreaking, dirty work with poor pay, picking cotton was worse than chopping cotton. Dad paid me according to performance and it was often lacking. If the growing season had been good, the cotton would grow tall, chest high to a man. This made the picking easier and from this came the expression, "We in high cotton." If the weather had been poor during the growing season, the cotton plants would be short and you would have bend over to pick it, giving you the backache. To prevent this, you could crawl along like a snake, one of which you might very well meet up with, eyeball to eyeball.

There was one hot afternoon I remember hearing screams and looked up to see dust and cotton stalks flying in the air. The "hands" ahead of me had come across a fat, big-around-as-a-man's arm, six-foot rattlesnake and was beating him into submission. I wasn't sure if rattlesnakes go to heaven or hell, but this one surely wasn't of this world any longer for they beat him to a pulp. I took the rest of the day off.

Cotton is worked entirely different today from the days of my youth. Manual labor has been replaced by motorized machines, the "hands" gone with the times. The mechanized cotton picker cares not one bit if the rows are long or the cotton is high, and it would run over any pesky rattlesnake. I haven't worked in a cotton patch in nearly fifty years and haven't missed it once, but I learned some valuable life lessons and have some stories to tell from the experience. That's almost like being in "high cotton" every day and much more comfortable. Today, the A/C is on high. Praise the Lord.

Nights Like This

Trains came through our town day and night. It was named Wadley, honoring the Central of Georgia Railway founder, William Wadley. A small place, it was no more than a widening in the road and almost exactly halfway between Savannah and Macon. Dad and I would sit on the front porch after supper and listen to the trains pass. We sat a good two miles from the tracks, but in the still of a quiet Georgia night their sounds were clear and pleasing. It was enough in those days.

The sounds of the passing trains would interrupt the bobwhite quails, whip-o-wills, and hoot owls we listened for from the woods across the road. We lived in the country on a dirt road and by that time of night and in those years, there was little else to hear. Sometimes we would hear a dog barking in the distance. My father had no use for a barking dog. On occasion our family dog would bark in the middle of the night. Dad never yelled at the dog to shut up like most folks would; he would ask a simple question, "What ails you?" I never heard the dog answer his question, but the dog always stopped barking. When I think back on it, I figure the dog either didn't know the answer to the question or was confused as to why he wasn't being yelled at. I do know the times Dad asked me the same question, "What ails you?" I too was pretty much at a loss for words, same as the dog.

Some folks claim whip-o-wills are calling their names with their sounds, "Whip-o-will, whip- o-will." Dad said they were calling out, "Plant your corn early, plant your corn early." Once again, I wasn't sure. What I do know is that I froze on February and March mornings getting land ready to plant corn. And I would freeze again on the porch after supper listening to the trains, bob whites, hoot owls, and the whip-o-wills calling out, "Plant your corn early, plant your corn early." I liked the sound but it was aggravating to a young boy with little patience for such things. "Plant your corn early, plant your corn early." I would have preferred to wait for warmer weather. I never once heard Dad ask those whip-o-wills, "What ails you?" I would have liked to know.

The fact is, we were never on the porch for the Nancy Hanks, a passenger train, on its return trip from Atlanta. Scheduled at 9:54 pm, it passed much too late for a farm family in those days. Dad went to bed every night at nine. My three sisters and I went soon after, or as soon as Mom could get us all ready for bed. There were times we could stay up later and watch a TV show. It was imperative, however, that we didn't disturb Dad. At no time did we ever want him to get up to quiet us down. It just wasn't done. I usually heard the Nancy Hanks at night from my bed. On warm nights, I slept next to an open window. There is something comforting about the sound on a peaceful Georgia night.

When Dad and I sat together on the porch listening, not much was said. He was quiet with his thoughts. I suppose it was his way of relaxing and ending a hard day's work. I never thought he had worries. He didn't appear to those nights, but he must have; he was responsible for a wife and four children. He always seemed so content just sitting there listening. Maybe that was his way of putting it all aside for a few minutes. All these many years ago, but as if it was just last night, I can recall vividly the sound of a match drug across a small wooden box and a flash of light when he lit a Pall Mall cigarette. Today that old dirt road has been paved and cars fly by. I could go back to that very same porch and again hear a train and a bobwhite quail just as we did all those years ago, but it wouldn't be the same.

There aren't many folks today who can be content with only the sounds of the forest and the trains. Much too busy, much too much else to see and do, this modern world is a noisy place. So many noises and we want more, but none can ever replace what I have lost. Nothing can replace listening to the night with your Dad. I haven't lost the memory though, and for that I am thankful.

❦ 5 ❧

Teenager

Wadley High School

Higher Education

Wadley High School was a two-story brick building with a large hallway down the center. There were stairs on each side of the hall; one was for going up, the other for coming down. However, when the last bell rang, both were one way down filled with escaping teenagers as afternoons were calling and much of life isn't found in books.

The building served as home for grades eight through twelve. Going to the eighth grade was like being in high school. You were with the older kids. Mama took me to JC Penney and Sears and Roebuck in Augusta for new clothes. I went from jeans and tennis shoes to the usual outfit for high schooling, dress pants and lace up leather shoes. I wasn't a little kid anymore, and the change made me feel grown. Unfortunately, the new wardrobe wasn't as comfortable, offering a hint of the inevitable discomforts of growing up.

The building had classrooms for science, English, typing, math, history, and home economics. There was a library and a science lab, which had a dual purpose. When teenage boys had behavior issues and teacher reprimands bounced off the boys' thick skulls, a "meeting" was held in the lab. There they tried another part of the anatomy which produced an amazing success rate. Behind the high school there was a separate building that housed agriculture and shop classes. It also served as town cannery in the summer. The smoking tree was nearby. This was the sixties; today canneries are rare and smoking trees are extinct due to Georgia's smoking ban on all campuses.

There was a gymnasium, tennis courts, football and baseball fields for athletics. Our teams were oddly nicknamed the Green Dragons. If we had been the Green Hound Dogs or the Green Mules, we might have had a live mascot, but green dragons were rare. I don't think I ever saw one. I saw a pink elephant once, but that story is unrelated to sports.

The total number of students approximated at any one time was one hundred and twenty-five. Eighth grade classes averaged forty, but by the twelfth grade some had moved away and some had dropped out. A few found themselves in a family way and married. My senior class, considered large, numbered twenty-three. The following year class was only thirteen. Too small for a quality education some might say; they would be wrong.

I was a good student but will confess to receiving one failing mark, an "F" in deportment, proper behavior being considered an equal to "book learning." It was the oddest thing. I made some smart aleck remark to my home room teacher while she called roll. She said, "Allen, I will mark down your deportment grade for that."

I replied, "I don't care if you give me an F."

She was good as her word and mine. She gave me an "F." When she passed out report cards, a note to my parents was attached that read, "Allen got an F in deportment because he said he didn't care."

I didn't, but my Mother did. I was immediately put on restriction for ninety-nine years.

Corporal punishment was in play all through high school. I was busted three times. The first time was by the science teacher, Mr. Barium. One day during a short break just before lunch, he called eight or ten of us boys up to the front of the class, lined us up along the blackboard and went down the line swinging, a lick each with emphasis. I'm still not sure what we did. He was an odd man with discipline. Second time, I was busted for going to Leo's gas station for a Coke and a Moon Pie after lunch. Under no circumstance did a student leave campus without permission. There was a trio of friends with me. My explanation to Mr. Simpson, the principal, that I was only driving the getaway car didn't cut any ice with him. Take ten licks or go home; I took the licks. It wasn't bad; he was a kindly man and his heart wasn't in it. Third time was by Mr. Martinez, the Ag teacher. He took us on a field trip to a cow lot. Once in the corral, I stepped and went knee deep in muddy cow manure. My remark of displeasure with this was a loud, "Good God Almighty!"

Apparently, he was offended by my choice of words. Back in class, I pled my case based on a Constitutional right to use those exact words whenever you were knee deep in manure. He didn't buy it. Three hard licks, holy smokes, he meant it. If I had been a wiser boy, I would have called Immigration and Naturalization Service and reported him. His name sounded fishy and he was from Texas, or so he said.

My mother offered me advice each time this happened: "Straighten up and fly right," whatever that meant. I tried but mostly failed. After all, I was a thick-skulled teenager. Maybe she should have affected that other part of the anatomy.

I don't mean for my school to sound less than it was; we had good teachers and one hundred percent support from the community. It was small without the resources of larger schools, but I learned, did well on my Scholastic Aptitude Test, and was accepted to the University of Georgia in December of my senior year. Others did the same, went to college and became fine citizens. Some others didn't study much at all but became fine citizens anyway, which proves, without a doubt, education isn't just books or found only in a big fancy school. A community of good folks helps - and maybe a touch of deportment training.

Almost Perfect

Life for a fourteen-year-old boy in the early 60's and all the years before were years of innocence. I knew of only one broken home in my entire town. I had been in the hospital once for hernia surgery, at five, or so they told me. My only memory was that there had been ice cream. A couple of kids in grammar school got ringworms, had their heads shaved, and wore stocking caps for a time. Other than childhood ailments like chickenpox or mumps, this is all I knew of sickness. My grandfather had died when I was two, but I had no memory of it, and so I had had no experience with death. I am sure there must have been bad things happening but I didn't know of them. News of the nation and of the world didn't factor into my life. My world was innocent and almost perfect.

My daily life was school and play. If I needed money, I worked for dad on the farm. I always needed money. Along with friends, I played in the woods, built forts and tree houses, dug caves, and dammed up streams. We played cowboys and Indians, cops and robbers, imitated Superman or Tarzan. We fished and hunted on occasion. I played ball but wasn't very good at it. Otherwise, my world was almost perfect.

Sunday afternoons my family visited both grandmas, Big Mama and Grandma Goodson, where we would be treated to Cokes or Kool-Aid. We also got cookies, pie, or cake. I don't remember ever not going to visit them. Sunday mornings we went to church for two hours; Sunday evening we went to church again for two more hours. Wednesday evenings we went to prayer meeting. Thursday evenings there was Royal Ambassadors, called RA's. That's a lot of church for a young boy. Otherwise, my world was almost perfect.

Up until this point in my life I had never heard my mother or father use a four-letter word. I very rarely had heard one at all and was surprised when I did. I had a best friend and free run of a three-hundred-and-sixty-acre farm. On one occasion we tried smoking corn silks and got busted for it. Incidentally, this was with the preacher's son. My mother was highly upset, but it didn't seem to bother dad much. I reckon he saw it as a coming-of-age thing for boys. I had a dog and cows and chickens. I had three sisters. Otherwise, my world was almost perfect.

In 1963 I was in the eighth grade, in the high school building. I was growing up, my life was changing, and it was cool. It was an exciting time. I learned older boys had a driver's license, a car, and full-time girlfriends. I began to like girls. I had my eye on this pretty redhead who was getting curvy. She looked great in sweaters, but she didn't have eyes for me. Rejection in the eighth grade is a miserable thing for a young boy. Otherwise, my world was almost perfect.

That year I had a pretty school teacher, named Ms. Kitchens. One afternoon just after lunch, the principal walked in the classroom unexpectedly and announced that the President had been shot. It was November 22, 1963, a Friday. Ms. Kitchens began to cry. It was the first time I ever saw a grown person cry. The room was total silence except for her crying. A boy near me half whispered, "I'm glad the n*gger lover got shot." His remark troubled me but I said nothing. Between sobs Ms. Kitchens, the teacher, begin to tell us this was a terrible tragedy and President Kennedy was a great man. I didn't really know what to think except to know it felt wrong. I was fourteen and up to this moment had lived in an innocent world. In a few minutes the Principal came back and told us the President had died. We were all to go home, but this time, it was not with joy at a shortened school day. Otherwise, my life was perfect.

Fifty years later I have seen other things that trouble me as much as that terrible event did in 1963. I dislike the cruelty of man even more today. I was lucky; I had fourteen years of innocence. Not everyone gets that. I read the newspaper daily but I skip over the bad news. Stubbornly, I avoid reading incidences of cruelty as much as possible, for there is little I can do. What I try to do is treat family, friends, and folks as kind and as respectful as I know how. Maybe that will do some good in the spaces around me. Sometimes I miss the mark. Please pardon shortcomings in my life when I fail to sow kindness and respect. Otherwise it's a life almost perfect.

Glory, Glory to Georgia

It was a big deal. In October 1965 a high school friend received two tickets to the Georgia Tech – Navy football game in Atlanta and invited me to go. At fifteen years old, we were traveling one hundred and fifty miles from Wadley to Atlanta. The Nancy Hanks train would get us there in time for the game and get us back later that Saturday night. Such an opportunity was pure fantasy for two young boys from a small country town in southeast Georgia. It was not an invitation you declined.

Neither of us had been to a college football game; neither of us had been to any kind of game larger than Friday night football in rural Georgia, at the smallest of small schools. Our high school, the Wadley Green Dragons, as well as the schools we played, could barely field a team at all. This was well before consolidation of the 70's and 80's, when small schools were common. My friend and I were not football players, but we both enjoyed the games. I had made the high school basketball team my freshman and sophomore years and was quite good at basketball except for the dribbling and shooting. I rode the bench, but not to worry for those pine planks had been worn smooth by young marginal players just like me, long before my time.

At 8:58 am on Saturday, we boarded the Nancy Hanks with game tickets and money enough to eat lunch on the train. I can't tell you what I ate but we both drank Coke, the favored product of our state. If you saw anyone drinking a Pepsi, they were either Yankees or outside agitators. I do remember the meal was considered fine dining or at least fine dining for a country boy. It was served with cloth napkins; I had never heard of such a thing. After 186 miles we arrived in Atlanta at 1:00 pm. Then a bus took us from the train station to Grant Field on the Georgia Tech campus.

There were more than forty thousand people at the game. When the old Ramblin' Wreck, a 1930 Model A Sport Coupe, Tech's official mascot drove out on the field, the crowd went wild. My country boy eyes opened wide taking it all in. In the game Tech destroyed Navy 37 to 16, a lot of points in the day when teams ran more and passed less. The offense was led by quarterback Kim King and a running back named Lenny Snow. In 1965 Georgia Tech had been THE football program in the state for years, but Georgia was coming on strong. I had no allegiance to either state school at the time, but later during my senior year in high school I applied to the University of Georgia and became a Georgia Bulldog for life. (My college career ended up very similar to my basketball career. I was good at college except for the studying and attending class.)

The Nancy Hanks took us home that night from the city of Atlanta to our small country home. This one day trip is a memory that I think was a turning point in my life. I had seen a big-time college football game; I had visited a big city; I had eaten with cloth napkins, and I had made a round trip of three hundred and fifty miles in one day. It opened my eyes and changed my view of the world. Outside of Wadley and the Green Dragons there was a big world to be discovered. I can't be certain, but I believe this was the day I became a wanderer.

And to hell with Georgia Tech.

Teen Driver

Time crawls along like molasses in our youth. We want to be older. We are eager to say we are four and a half, not just four. We can't wait to be ten, and then thirteen, and sixteen, and eighteen, and twenty-one. Suddenly one day we find ourselves fifty or sixty and think, whoa, slow down. Time gets away.

Of these ages, sixteen was the one I hoped would hurry up the most. Sixteen meant a driver's license and freedom, and a chance to explore my world, small as it was. Up to that point, I had been out of the state of Georgia twice, to Washington, DC, and Pompano Beach, FL, on family vacations. I had been to Millen and Vidalia to visit relatives, Louisville, Swainsboro, and Augusta for shopping and doctor appointments. My parents drove, but I didn't approve of their driving (the molasses thing) and figured I could do better. I could get anywhere faster than either one of them.

Being a farm boy, I started driving tractors as soon as my feet would reach the pedals. My driving skills were honed to perfection well before I was old enough for a driver's license, or so I thought. I should point out here for the uninformed that tractors are built heavily and are much more immune to bumps and bruises than something like a car fender. Ditches meant nothing; you could accidently run into one and drive right out with only the ditch and your pride the worst for it. Furthermore, the top speed of a tractor going downhill with a tail wind is about twenty-five miles per hour. Cars go much faster. All this aside, I thought I was a very good driver, certainly as good or better than my parents, clearly ready for a driver's license, the family car, and the highway. I shouldn't have to tell you: teenage boys are the smartest humans on the planet and their parents are dummies. This is a universal fact; ask any male teenager if you don't believe me.

I first introduced our family car to a ditch when I had a learner's permit. During my sophomore year in high school, I was trying to become a basketball star to win the favors of pretty girls. Practice was at night and we lived a couple miles from school, all dirt road from home to the gym. Rather than have to drop me off and then pick me up again in two hours, Dad thought I would be fine to drive myself. I arrived at practice in fine shape but coming home there was a problem. There was one curve between school and home, ONE. Naturally, I took it too fast and the left rear of the car slid into the ditch with a crunch. I crawled out of the car and turned to notice that it was at a severe and odd angle, the left rear deep in the ditch and the front end pointed up in the air as if looking to the heavens. I, too, looked to the heavens, hoping and praying for some Divine intervention, but none was forthcoming, so I begin to walk. The walk wasn't my worry. It was the getting home, waking my father, and telling him his car was in the ditch. He frowned and said one word to me, "Boy." I never knew that one word had so much meaning.

The next time I crumpled a fender, I was a fully licensed driver with a carload of my pals. We were riding the dirt roads, having a blast as only teenagers can, when I rounded a sharp curve way too fast (again) and found myself looking straight at a car coming from the other direction. If not for my cat-like reflexes, there would have been a head on collision. I managed to steer the car hard right and avoid the oncoming vehicle but, unfortunately, not the six-foot clay bank that ran along right side of the dirt road. I heard "crunch" for the second time in my young life and watched the other car carry on safely down the road. After checking that everyone was OK, I reviewed the situation. On a positive note, this time it was the right front crumpled, not the left rear as before. Not sure why I thought that was a positive, but I did. Better yet, I had three good friends to ride home with and support me while I explained to Dad. "Not so fast, fender bender breath!" my good buddies exclaimed, "Take us home; we can't help you with Mr. Emmett."

I can't blame them. In certain situations, sixteen-year-old boys are scared to death of parents. So, I faced Dad alone and got the usual frown and disapproving "Boy." It wasn't so bad though, maybe because I was more experienced this time.

I bent more fenders and worse over the years but only those two times as a teenager with the family car. Although not a parent myself, I suppose a dad, after the disappointment of his child making a mistake, feels blessed it wasn't worse. Today, far from being an inexperienced teenager, I still screw up. I still hear Dad's voice in my head, "Boy," but to hear it now, out loud as I did as a briefly humbled teenager, would be an undeserved blessing.

The Great Watermelon Caper

Confession is good for the soul, or so it says in First John 1:9. My soul can use some work, and even though a public confession is difficult, I intend to own up to the error of my ways, here and now. Well, not quite now. Bear with me, I need to share some background and to get up the nerve.

Back in my youth, my family was known for growing watermelons. My father, my uncle, and my grandfather were considered the premier growers of melons far and wide. I heard more than a few people say, "A Goodson watermelon is the best."

Watermelons were good business with lots of cash transactions. Cash was hard to come by in those days for everyone, especially hard for a sixteen-year-old farm boy. I was cash strapped all the time, and the need for funds increased tenfold when I turned sixteen and acquired a driver's license. I suppose perceptive readers will anticipate where I am going with this story.

This despicable act I am soon to confess to occurred due to a Billy Joe Royal dance at the National Guard Armory in Dublin, GA. Whenever Billy Joe Royal played within sixty miles of home, word got around quickly. Young folks now may have to Google Billy Joe, but I can tell you with complete assurance he was all the rage at the time. He was Georgia born and had made it big with several popular hits including "Down in the Boondocks" and "Cherry Hill Park."

The love of my life at the time expressed her interest in going and what Mona Lott wanted, Mona Lott got. I, of course, was in need of financial aid to make it happen. Dad was always willing to fork out a few dollars and the loan of the family car for me to have a good time, assuming I had worked during the week. But for this event I would need at least twenty dollars, an unheard amount for "teenage gallivanting," as he called it. I checked my slush fund, zero, my savings, zilch, my accounts receivable, none, and all my friends were broke and of no account. I couldn't blame them though; broke was the common status for teenagers in the 60's. Things weren't looking good.

Like a thunder bolt, the solution hit me. Watermelons equal cash. I had helped Dad with the harvest every morning and had watched him peddle them around town, as well as sell them in the yard for buyers who drove out to the farm. There was a cigar box full of cash in the kitchen from those sold in the yard, but I knew better than to touch that. It would be stealing. However, I could fill the trunk of the car with Goodson melons, peddle them on the way to the dance, and therefore earn the cash to finance the aforementioned teenage frolic. Obviously, taking them from the patch without permission was the same as stealing, but my teenage mind was counting on some time with Mona and thinking stopped there.

I figured there were only two things that could go wrong with this plan. Loading a car trunk down with watermelons causes the rear end to sit lower to the ground than the front end. To local law enforcement this unlevel position indicated the hauling of illegal contraband, probably moonshine or whiskey, both of which were highly frowned upon in the Deep South in those days. The trip involved me traveling through Bartow, GA, and Wrightsville, GA, where there were sure to be local authorities, as well as county sheriffs and the Georgia State Patrol on the open highway. I wasn't hauling illegal contraband, but a load of watermelons could lead to interrogation and questions like, "Where you get them melons, boy?"

The other thing that could go wrong was Dad finding out I took the melons. If he found out the next day when he went to the watermelon patch, there would be trouble, but not nearly as much as if the news came from the authorities. Dad was a meticulous man and had a sixth sense when it came to his cows or crops. He walked the watermelon patch every morning and selected the best melons to sell. I believe he knew every melon and would likely spot the theft. He probably would even notice his own car's tire tracks. Car tracks in a watermelon patch meant theft, but I was a teenager and, like many thieves, stupid.

I avoided the authorities that night, as well as my dad's wrath; however, recently I have come to believe that dad knew of my thievery, remembered his youth, and decided to give me a pass. I have it from an excellent source that he had done the same. He had stolen watermelons from his father's patch to finance his own teenage gallivanting, and even went a step further, for there had been a chicken included with his goods for sale. I swear I never stole a chicken, dad's or otherwise.

Things to note here: your parents were young once and, regardless of the times, teenagers are teenagers. Lastly, the apple doesn't fall far from the tree. There, I confessed; I feel better already.

A Young Man's Spring

Early spring 1968, a junior in high school, seventeen - there hasn't been a better time in my life. Every day after school and on Saturdays I was on the tractor. The tractor was a brand new Farmall 806 and my job was to harrow the fields. At the time I didn't appreciate it, but there is nothing more therapeutic than working the land. For hours I would cross the fields tilling up new earth in the warm Georgia sun, having only to look back every few minutes to check the harrow and my work. The smell of the freshly turned soil and the constant hum of the engine made for a relaxing and peaceful experience. My love of farming came from this farm chore.

For my work, I would be paid a few dollars and the use of the Ford family sedan on Friday or Saturday night, sometimes both. I was happy with the arrangement, but sometimes Dad was not. He disapproved of me returning home with only a small amount of gas left in the tank, a habit I couldn't seem to break. Early mornings he would walk in my bedroom, pass on some fatherly advice, "Do not bring my car home on empty," and walk out. He was a man of few words and I was a slow learner. Luckily, he wasn't a hard man; in fact, he was pretty generous for a Georgia farmer with a family of four to raise. Years later when I thought back on it and heard some stories about him as a young boy, I came to believe he remembered what it was to be a boy of seventeen. His childhood had been during the Depression and when he was only a year or so older than I, he was called to war. He was among the first Americans to experience the war, for on December 7, 1941, he was a sailor stationed at Pearl Harbor. What that can do to a man, to a young boy as he was at the time, is unimaginable to me. I reckon a man who goes through anything like that knows the tragedy of a lost youth. I think he did his best to make sure I had a good one.

One particular week I worked hard and had done as Dad said. It was Friday night and I had a date. Dad always adjusted my pay to what he thought I needed for the occasion. He allowed for some discussion about the amount, but it was mostly the same. If I had a date and the family car, he would give me five bucks, less if I was going with the boys and not taking the car. (A wise man, he knew seventeen-year-olds with too much money was inviting trouble.) Younger readers may not realize this, but in 1968 five dollars made for a nice date. I could buy four gallons of gas for one dollar, go to a movie, and have money left over to buy hamburgers, french fries, and cokes. That is, of course, assuming we went to a movie; sometimes we just cruised around and my plan would be getting to second base. Unfortunately, I wasn't a Romeo and most often was left stranded on first.

For a while I dated an "older woman," a pretty blonde from a neighboring town ten miles away. I was a junior boy dating a senior girl. My pals thought this was cool. Of course, I was thrilled. Not only that, she would come to the farm on afternoons and ride with me on the tractor. In those days tractors didn't have cabs, and seating was designed for one. She would sit on the fender or in my lap. I didn't mind where she sat and I guess she didn't either. The company of a pretty girl, whether seventeen or seventy is one of the best things life has to offer, and to a teenage boy it is pure heaven. The tractor was noisy, making it almost impossible to carry on a conversation, but I didn't care. I grinned a lot. She grinned back. We would ride back and forth across the field happy as only two teenagers can be, turning the earth with a disc harrow, and getting the land ready to plant. I am sure my focus wasn't the best, but the work got done. This was forty-five years before the song, "She thinks my tractor's sexy" came out. She was ahead of her time.

Whenever she was riding with me, Dad would drive by in his pickup and give me thumbs up, but I was not sure it was for the job I was doing or if he enjoyed seeing me have a good time. He was that kind of a father. In May my sweetheart graduated and was off to college. I had another year of high school and tractor driving to complete before college. For the thumbs up and the other things Dad did to make my youth a good one, I salute him. I hope I did some things along the way to pay him back.

6

Coming Home

Dad

Coming Home

My father was a cow man, as I have mentioned. He loved Herefords, the red ones with white faces. He only bought heifers; for city folk that means girl cows. When I asked him why, he said they were easier to work with than steers, possibly a fact that stretches across the entire animal kingdom, including humans. Steers are boy cows with their anatomy slightly altered, if you get my drift. This "alteration" keeps boy cows from chasing girl cows twenty-four/seven. He also said heifers fattened up quicker than steers. I won't add any smart remark to that last sentence for it would surely not be taken well by female readers. Nobody needs that kind of trouble.

Dad's gentle nature worked especially well with cows. Cows are not the smartest animals in the world, but they quickly learn who serves dinner. In fact, anytime they saw his truck, they would come running. Whenever he wanted to move them to a new pasture, they would follow his truck. He could also herd them with arm and hand gestures, sometimes with a firm, never loud, vocal command "Hey-aah." Over the years a few heifers ignored his guidance and the guilty ones would then be named "Old Fool." Dad advised me there was one in every herd. It seems to be like that with people as well.

I left home at eighteen after graduating from high school and had been away for five years when I decided to come home and farm with him. Growing up, we had a fair to middling father-son relationship and I had gotten in more than my share of youthful trouble. When I did, he would shake his head and mutter, but to his credit he never called me "Young Fool," although I am sure I had given him ample reason to do so.

Back home we soon got in a groove working together. Then one late winter day, driving along the dirt road that split the farm, Dad looked out over the field surveying the cows and said to me, "One is missing. We better check." I had no idea how he knew one had wandered astray from the hundred in the herd. Ten could be missing and I would be none the wiser. Dad pulled over to the side of the road and parked beside the fifty-acre field. Wheat planted there was shining from the morning dew.

Although the herd was usually in the feedlot, we had let them out there to graze and stretch their legs. This was done occasionally, though only for a few days at a time as the green grass was rich and they could eat themselves sick. Dad had parked by a gate where a hedgerow began. Running three fourths the way across the field, it then fanned out to become a wet weather pond. Half way between the road and the wet weather pond was an old home site. The house was gone, but a rotting paddock and a well, supposedly covered with boards, remained. I assumed Dad thought the cow to be there.

We walked along the hedgerow hoping to find her safe but, unfortunately, found her in the well. She was standing in water up to her belly. Luckily, the water wasn't deeper or she would have drowned. Up until this point in my life Dad had always had the answer for any problem that arose. I had lived my entire young life depending on him for just that. To this day I am not sure if he didn't have an answer or if he was testing me, for he looked at me and asked, "How are we going to get her out?" I thought for few seconds and the solution came with surprising ease.

I replied, "We can get Mr. Virgil to bring his wrecker and I will go down on the cable, put the belt around her, and lift her out."

Mr. Virgil ran the local Gulf gas station we did business with, and he was always ready to help out in a pinch.

Dad stayed with the young heifer while I drove the truck to town to fetch help. Mr. Virgil realized the need for urgency, dropped what he was doing, and followed me back. He backed his wrecker as close as possible to the well and I climbed aboard. He moved a lever and down I went. It all worked perfectly and I found myself astraddle the poor cow. She was shivering, scared to death, but didn't move. I managed to get enough slack in the cable to hook the belt under her belly and up around her sides. With the belt and cable secure, I waved a thumbs up to Mr. Virgil. He started the winch and slowly lifted me and the heifer up and out of the well, pretty as you please. Back on dry ground, I dismounted, loosened the belt, and she walked away as if nothing had happened.

For a few minutes we watched to be sure she was not hurt, and then Dad, the man I had depended on for everything for all those years, turned to me and said, "Much obliged."

He then for the first time shook my hand, man to man.

That day I should have thanked him for the handshake and told him how much it meant to me. There are other things I should have told him, but time got away. Maybe he is reading this Up There. Maybe he has always known. But just in case, "Thanks, Dad."

A Southern Sailor

It was early December 1991, and Honolulu was decorated for the holiday season. Along with a couple thousand other old sailors and soldiers, Dad was in Hawaii to commemorate the fiftieth anniversary of the attack on Pearl Harbor, which took place on December 7, 1941. My mother and one of my sisters had come along.

The other guest in Hawaii that week was the USS Missouri, the last battleship to be built by the United States. On the deck of this battleship, standing before General Douglas MacArthur, the Japanese signed an unconditional surrender to Allied Forces, ending World War II. One morning Mom and my sister decided to go shopping, so I asked Dad, "What do you want to do?"

He said, "I would like to go on the Missouri and see where the peace treaty was signed."

Normally, this wouldn't have been a problem, but Dad was having difficulties with mobility and needed the aid of a wheelchair. A least we could go to the ship, and, if we couldn't get on, he would get to see it up close. So we loaded up the rental car and took off to Pearl Harbor. That is when the magic started to happen.

A very young and sharp-looking Marine greeted us at the Pearl Harbor gate. I explained to him that Dad had been at Pearl Harbor during the attack and wished to see the USS Missouri. The Marine took a few seconds to look me over. Then he looked at Dad, who was wearing his Pearl Harbor Survivors garrison cap. Without asking for further ID, the Marine said, "Sir, go anywhere you wish, sir." He saluted. Dad returned the salute. I reckon this young Marine and the Navy figured some men have earned certain rights.

And so, we did go where we wished, looking for the Missouri. Things were in our favor: the crowd was very small and I was able to drive the car right up to the ship. However, chances of going onboard didn't look good, as the gang plank was steep and long. I wheeled Dad closer anyway, so that he could at least get a good look at the ship from the dock. Another young sailor came up and asked if he could be of help. I told him about Dad being a survivor and wanting to go aboard to see where the treaty was signed. The young sailor must have signaled or something, for the next thing I saw was two more young sailors come running. In an instant, they picked Dad up, wheelchair and all. They carried him up the gangplank, set him on the deck of the Missouri, and saluted him. Dad returned their salute.

A plaque mounted in the deck marks the spot where Japanese officials signed the unconditional surrender ending World War II. Dad and I went straight to that spot. The two of us were alone there for at least ten minutes. Dad would look down at the plaque for a few moments, then look up and out over the harbor, and then back down at the plaque. He repeated this several times. Not one word was said. I have no idea what he was thinking... I assumed he was thinking of the war fifty years gone by. I had no idea what to say. My father was a quiet man. When he spoke, it was important to listen. I waited for words. He finally looked at me and said, "Let's go to the bow."

I rolled him out to the bow where we stopped by the edge of the ship to take in the view. On the calm, sunny day, Pearl Harbor had never looked better. From the bow, we saw the first tourists board this huge ship, about thirty children with three ladies. I assumed it was a class of 4th or 5th graders on a field trip. After a few minutes, one of the kids walked up to Dad with her brochure of the Missouri and asked Dad to autograph it. I supposed with his Survivor's cap and his white beard she thought he might be someone famous. He signed it and smiled. Then another child walked up, and another, and another, until he had signed the brochure for each one. The kids were smiling, Dad was smiling, and I was about to burst with pride.

I wrote this story to tell you of the best Christmas gift I ever received, a truly wonderful morning with my dad. An intimate time between a son and a father. A morning I can't forget. I also wrote this story to tell you that every person ought to have moments in their lives when they are made to feel more than they are in their everyday lives, that they are special, that they have greatness.

My dad, Mr. Emmett as he was called, was a good father, a good husband, a good farmer, and a simple man. And that's enough, but that morning on the deck of the battleship, the USS Missouri, those thirty school kids thought he was much more than that.

So did I.

Color of a Cry

Once I attended a writer's workshop titled, "Tapping Your Creative Right Brain." It ran nine a.m. to five p.m. with a break for lunch. The published writer giving the workshop introduced himself, gave us a handout, and then followed with detailed verbal instruction. The handout read: The left brain is logical, sequential, rational, analytical, objective, and looks at parts. The right brain is random, intuitive, holistic, synthesizing, subjective, and looks at wholes.

Ten people attended the class, nine females ranging in age from fourteen to seventy--and me. The writer asked why we came. He pointed to me first and I answered, "I am the most left brained person in this room. I have lived my life using my left brain almost exclusively, and to be a better writer I understand I need to learn to use my creative mind better. "

After asking everyone's reason for attending, he explained we would do a number of writing exercises designed to better use our right brain. He further explained that the exercises would start with him presenting different types of stimuli; these included music, sounds, images, and smells. We would then have four to eight minutes to write what we felt. "Don't stop to edit, just write," he directed. After each exercise we would either read aloud in class or in smaller groups. We were instructed to reply to each, "Thanks for sharing." There was to be no critique at all. With some exercises I could take off and write and write until the time ran out, with others I could manage only a paragraph or two.

At the end of the day, we came to the last exercise. He gave us the choice of two subjects: 1. What sound does a rainbow make? or 2.What is the color of a cry? I chose the second. This is what I wrote:

Gray is the color of a cry. I learned this two years ago in the early fall after receiving a call from my middle sister explaining that Mama was sick and in the hospital. She went on in some detail, but my left brain kicked in and I told her not to worry. To calm her, I told her I was sure Mom would be fine and to please keep me posted. The very next day I received a call from my oldest sister, the call you never want to get. She was crying and having a hard time with the words. In short, the message was, "GET HOME FAST." My efficient left brain kicked into action. I booked flights with an itinerary to get me from an island in the middle of the Pacific Ocean to Augusta, GA, in record time.

I arrived the next day, late afternoon, with no problems. Entering the hospital, I spied my sisters and other family members having an early dinner. They brought me up to date on Mom's condition and we all went to her room. She was resting peacefully but unaware of our presence. We all sat quietly chatting a bit until one of the girls volunteered to spend the night there and further suggested we should all go home and get a good night's sleep.

The next morning, we four siblings returned to Mom's room after breakfast. The morning was full of family and visitors. An old friend of Mom's from high school stopped by. With tears in his eyes, he said Mom had been his first date. The morning was solemn but it went by fast. After a quick lunch, my three sisters and I and a niece returned to Mom's room.

I am not sure how it started but we begin to reminisce about our childhood. My baby sister told of the time we locked her in the chicken coop and would leave her there until Mama made us let her out for supper. We laughed and laughed with stories told and of memories relived. Unlike my boyhood years, I realized how fortunate I had been to have three sisters. And then amidst all this joy and laughter in the room, my niece, a nurse, (they know these things,) rushed to Mama's side. Right away I saw that Mama had taken her last breath. She was eighty-five. Neither side of my brain could process this, for it is a matter for the heart. I looked away staring at the wall, and thought simply, "gray."

The walls of Mama's room are gray. Gray is the color of a cry.

Mama's Closet

It is a mysterious thing how words or images can trigger thoughts. This morning, thoughts were triggered while ending a conversation with a friend, "Have a good day."

Meaning it wouldn't be a good day, she replied, "I am cleaning out closets today."

It should be said here that I am a poor housekeeper. Dust and the like, I can walk over and around with the least of worries. I do, however, dislike clutter, and so anything that sits around for a length of time must go, either to the trash bin or, if it has any value, to the Salvation Army.

My life has been a series of many moves; apparently, I am a wanderer and part gypsy. Clutter is a hindrance for my chosen lifestyle. While some find value in things and in keeping them, I rarely do. My most prized possessions are a couple of large manila envelopes filled with old pictures.

When my friend mentioned she was cleaning closets, I recalled the last time I cleaned one out. It was the day after Mama's funeral. There is not one good thing about saying goodbye to a parent. I have done it twice now. The funeral was hard, hard. The closet cleaning was harder. My three sisters and I met at our childhood home the morning after and sat around the kitchen table where we had eaten thousands of meals, all prepared and served by Mama. There was some business about the estate, which went smoothly. There was discussion about things and who should get them and who might want them. All this went very well and when it came my turn to say what I wanted, I said, "A few pictures."

The property was to be sold and everything had to go. Unlike me, Mama rarely threw anything away. I think this is common with Depression babies. It was our task this day to sort through it all and prepare the house for sale. We all wandered around, not quite knowing where to start, or even if we could get it together enough to start. We began by taking family pictures off the wall, I noticed that there were many more pictures of grandchildren and great grandchildren than any of us four siblings. The circle of life, I thought.

After the pictures, we each went to a closet. I opened one that Mom had used for storage. In it were some of Dad's old clothes, his Hawaiian shirts, some khaki pants, and two suits. He had been gone years and up until an hour before, I wouldn't have understood why Mama hadn't disposed of them. I understood now.

In the bottom of the closet was a stack of children's games; Monopoly was on top and I pulled it out. Fifty or more years old, it was full of memories of games played with sisters and friends. A Parcheesi game was next but, with emotions building, I left it in place. Next to it was a small plain brown paper bag with the word "save" written in pencil across it. Inside was a cheap costume jewelry necklace. I had no idea where this necklace came from or whose it might have been. Frankly, it wasn't much but I stuck it in my pocket without saying a word to my sisters. After an hour or so, we all decided we could not do this, not on this day. Some time needed to pass.

The time will come when someone will go through my things. I can't tell you where or when it will be, but if I have any say-so, it will be someplace I consider paradise and it will be a long, long time coming. This person will find among my prized possessions a cheap costume jewelry necklace in a small brown paper bag and if they have read this story, they will know of its importance to me.

Mama wrote "save" and so I did.

Time Gets Away

I am pretty sure it was just yesterday, or maybe this past week, or last month, or last year, or ten years ago. I can't be sure of the time, for my memory is poor. I can't even remember with clarity what I had for breakfast, but I know with certainty I was once young. It couldn't have been so long ago; it must have been a recent past. My driver's license says I am seventy. How is that possible? I was young not so very long ago.

I remember being four years old and fighting with my three sisters when they were two, six, and seven. We fought over games of Monopoly, over who got the top hat piece. We fought over Parcheesi and Chinese Checkers.

"Mama, Allen is cheating," was a common refrain.

We fought over their admittance every time I built a new fort. We fought until Mama had had enough and put her foot down. That much is clear to me, and it wasn't so long ago.

I remember waking up on a Christmas morning and to my youthful delight finding a Lionel train under the Christmas tree, the engine and cars so blue it would hurt your eyes. Another year it was a Daisy BB gun, and another year a brand-new bicycle with shiny chrome handle bars. Santa Claus and the Tooth fairy were real as real can be. Santa drank the milk and ate the cookies; the Tooth Fairy left a quarter. That was real money, easily enough to buy a coke and a candy bar. Those were the days and they weren't so long ago. I can't be a senior citizen.

I remember following Dad, his right-hand man Mr. Albert, and the older boys around the watermelon patch early June and July mornings just about daylight. The watermelon vines were wet with dew that would soak my pants legs nearly to my waist. I remember being so small I could barely carry a melon and I dropped a few. It didn't matter much; the short drop from a boy my size to a cushiony sand bed of a watermelon patch rarely busted one.

Dad would cut one open every now and again to be sure his thumping was on the mark. When he did, I was free to scoop out a huge chunk of the heart which was about the best tasting thing in the world, those days. I would then be wet below the waist from morning dew and wet above the waist from watermelon juice, which apparently attracted deer flies with their nasty bites. I remember all that clearly. How was that over a half century ago?

I remember my twenties, quite possibly the best twenties a country boy could have. I was a student at the University of Georgia until studying got in the way of fun. I fell in love two times, first with a petite blonde from the big city of Atlanta and later with a funny talking country girl, both wonderful Southern Belles. Some say I should have married one of those girls. I say I had already made them miserable, so why do more harm? I was young and foolish. I remember it all so well. It couldn't have been that long ago.

My uncle asked me when I was in my thirties, "How old are you?" Uncles are not required to know this information and so I told him I was thirty-two. He, being a very wise man, went on to say that the thirties are your best years. You have lived and learned, and you are still young enough to do anything physically that you want. I expect he was right about that. I remember our conversation clearly; it seems like yesterday. How could that have been thirty-something years ago?

My uncle didn't tell me about time flying by. Somewhere in my late thirties a time warp thing kicked in and the last years have got behind me faster than a speeding bullet. I have no idea how that happened and I don't like it much that it has. If I had a wish, I would wish for time to slow down. I long to see more sunrises and share many more laughs with good friends. Maybe even wake up to see a Lionel train under a Christmas tree just for me, one so blue it will hurt your eyes. Those were the days and I was so very young.

7

Visiting

Wadley Main Street 1949

Jefferson County

Jefferson County, Georgia, is the place of my birth and home for my youthful years. At eighteen I eagerly left it, high school behind me, for Athens and the University of Georgia. I did not know at the time what a huge impact "place" has in our formative years. The air and dirt become woven into who we become. Now, over six decades later, I know. The lessons and experience of growing up there have helped pave my way.

Jefferson County, five hundred and thirty square miles in size, is located in southeast Georgia and surrounded by eight counties: Richmond, McDuffie, Warren, Glascock, Washington, Johnson, Emanuel, and Burke. Oddly, it resembles a peanut standing on its end, and maybe it should, considering the acres of peanuts planted in its soil.

From Louisville, the county seat, it is a forty-six-mile drive to Augusta, eighty-five to Macon, one hundred nineteen to Savannah, and one hundred forty-eight to Atlanta. It is as rural as rural can be. East of Jefferson County, some fifty miles as the crow flies, is the South Carolina border. I asked one. He seemed trustworthy.

There are six incorporated cities, towns really, smaller than any city, but larger than a village. Louisville has a population of 2,493; Wrens 2,187; Wadley 2,061; Stapleton 438; Bartow 286; and Avera 246. Numerous additional communities no more than a wide place in the road dot the countryside, though these have yet to incorporate. The total population for the county according to the 2015 census is 16,106.

The settlement of Jefferson County began in 1758, on the Ogeechee River, eight miles southeast of current day Louisville and seventeen years before the American Revolutionary War. George Galphin, an Irishman, established an Indian trading post which he named Galphinton. It is now known as "Old Town."

Eight years later, Galphin and his business partner John Rea brought a bill before the young colony's General Assembly to bring farming and industry to the area, and to provide a buffer from Indians to the "civilized" world of the Georgia and South Carolina coast. With the Governor's support the Assembly authorized 50,000 acres and 1815 pounds sterling to cover cost. A new township was born, northeast of Galphinton, and was named Queensborough in honor of Queen Anne, sovereign ruler of England, Scotland, and Ireland from 1702 to 1714.

An advertisement was placed in the Belfast News-Letter by Rea to encourage Irish immigrants. It read: "The land I have chosen is good for wheat, and any kind of grain, indigo, flax, and hemp will grow to great perfection, and I do not know any place better situated for a flourishing township than this place will be. People that live on the low land near the sea are subject to fever and agues, but high up in the country it is healthy [with] fine springs of good water. The winter is the finest in the world, never too cold, very little frost and no snow." *

A few hundred made the arduous journey to develop the settlement.

America gained its final independence in 1783 with the Treaty of Paris, and in 1786 the young Georgia state government in Savannah decided to establish a permanent capital between there and Augusta. Three men were sent to find a site. Requirements: An area of friendly, peace loving Indians, good drinking water, and a high place above swampy vapors. The chosen place was named Louisville after King Louis XVI of France, for he had been an important ally to America during the Revolutionary War.

The Georgia Assembly met in Louisville on February 20, 1796, and created Jefferson County, named after the third U.S. President Thomas Jefferson, one hundred and fifty-three years before I was born. It remained the capital until 1807. During that time there were five Governors: Irwin, Jackson, Emanuel, Tattnall, and Milledge; fifteen counties formed; the current Georgia seal adopted; and the University of Georgia was established. There you have it, a brief history of the beginning. There is much more.

Geographically speaking, the US Highway # 1 traverses Jefferson County from the north to the south, dividing it into almost equal halves, east and west. History tells us this highway constructed in the 1920's was the main motor vehicle corridor in the United States upon being built. It follows the Atlantic Ocean closely from Maine to Florida except in the Carolina's where it veers inland through Augusta, GA, and on to Jacksonville, FL, and there meets the ocean again.

This inland direction allowed Yankee travelers of the day to visit my home county. And why not? It held oak-lined streets, white painted homes neatly kept, and the friendliest folks this side of the Mason Dixon line, Southern fried chicken and sweet tea served daily, juicy peaches and mouthwatering watermelons in season. In the 1960's, bypass roads were built around Louisville and Wadley. This allowed the Yankees to drive around our towns at such a speed they forgot to wave. ("Thou shalt wave" is the eleventh commandment in the South. It's what we do.) The town's police rarely bothered the Yankees, those days. Even when they did and had lightened their pockets of a few dollars, they always sent speeders on their way with a cheerful drawl, " Y'all come back, ya hear."

As our great country grew in wealth and population and time went by, US Highway 1 lost traffic to an improved US 301 and then later to a newly constructed Interstate 95. Loss of tourist traffic did not matter since agriculture and timber has sustained us well in Jefferson County.

I been gone for thirty plus years in the pursuit of life, but the love of a pretty blonde brought me back. It's good here, this modern-day Jefferson County. Folks know me and know my family. They speak kindly. It is what folks in small places do.

"Hi ya doing?"

"I'm fine, how you?"

The answer to these friendly greetings rarely matters; it is that you were spoken to. There is gravity and comfort in that.

*Population statistics from U.S. Census 2015

*Scotch-Irish," "Real Irish," and "Black Irish": Immigrants and Identities in the Old South by Kerby A. Miller

Photo credit: David Benbennick - Wikipedia

Visiting

On a recent trip home, my cousin and I did a town tour. We drove around and stopped at places where memories were the strongest. We talked about people and of events from the past. It was bittersweet, though mostly pleasurable as our memories are good ones. We drove by houses where once a upon a time we could name everyone who lived there. On this day some fifty years later, we weren't so sure.

One of the highlights of our tour was the school. The high school building is gone, torn down, progress or money saving seems to have been the reason, but the grammar school, lunchroom, and gym are still there. The gym has been dressed up with a new exterior and we found it open. Before we went in, I asked my cousin testing our memory, "Do you remember how many rows of seats make up the stands?"

He replied, "eight."

I thought it must have been much larger than that and said, "twelve."

Not surprisingly, there were only six rows per side, a testament to our poor memory, and the entire inside, though remarkably unchanged, had shrunk, or so it seemed. Didn't matter for on game nights the whole town squeezed inside and cheered us on. My cousin and I walked out on the court and memories came back. My entire high school athletic career, or lack thereof, had played out right here. "I rode the pines" and sat far from the coach, which meant the only chance of me playing was in a blow out, either by us or by the other guys. As poor a player as I was, I still practiced hard, ran wind sprints, and laps just like the starters did. It all seemed so important then and it still was on this visit but for different reasons. High school years are full of youthful dreams. Youth gets away, but dreams are to be held on to.

Next to the gym is the playground we used when we were in grammar school. At recess, dodgeball, tether ball, and softball were what we had played the most. I saw a pecan tree that I remember being first base during softball games. It wasn't so on this day, but years ago the base paths and the playing fields were worn clean of grass by the Keds and PF Flyers on the feet of children playing ball. Just across the way was the sixth and seventh grade building, glass windows now boarded up. For a few minutes I stood there and remembered the name of every teacher I had had through twelve grades, a remarkable feat since there are times now, I can't remember the name of someone I met yesterday. That says something about the imprint teachers have on the young.

As we loaded up and left the school, I thought of something that I would never WANT to do. I said to my cousin, "Want to go to the cemetery?"

He said, "Yes."

I had been to the cemetery before, but not sure I had ever "wanted to go" as I did on this occasion.

Our family plot had been bought and paid for by my grandfather, John Franklin Goodson. He, my grandmother, my parents, my cousin's parents, and another cousin, all who left us too soon, are laid to rest there. We stood there silently, viewing family names in granite, each of us with our own memories, our own sadness. We walked the entire cemetery, coming across names we had known. We talked of memories and stories about these people. We came across a few we didn't know at all and talked about who they might possibly have been.

Visiting a cemetery is unlike any other experience. It is bittersweet times ten. In our daily lives we think of those there, of happy times shared, but to see their names and life dates etched in stone feels so final and sad. Looking at a marker, reading the full name and calculating the length of a life from carved numbers is a complete confirmation that they are gone.

I am not sure why I wanted to go there that day; emotionally, it was a hard thing. My heart was saddened and my eyes were wet. Maybe I went for them because they lived. What I do know is that living is hard, but mine has been made smoother and sweeter by those souls resting there. I hope they know that their lives mattered.

Glory Days

It is an irregular shaped piece of land, almost a rectangle. If it is larger than four acres, I would be surprised. Today it would be called an Athletic Complex or something similar; in the sixties our world wasn't complex, so it was simply the football and baseball field.

This slice of Georgia dirt, like so many others around the South, was a place for games played by high schoolers. Adults reminisce about those years gone by and their "glory days" of athletic endeavors played out on similar fields. This facility is still bordered on the north by a road that was in my day paved only beyond the baseball field. Today the road has been paved in its entirety and runs for a mile or so into the countryside. Paving of dirt roads is a sign of progress, or so some say. I am not so sure.

A train track runs along the east side on ground lower than the field itself. It was the Louisville and Wadley Railroad incorporated in 1872, though the name has changed over the years. During my teen years it came by daily and, on occasion, interrupted a game being played. The west boundary of this athletic arena was cropland. Errant balls could land at any time in corn, wheat, or soybeans. On the south side there was a small thin line of trees partly shielding two homes from view.

I found myself there recently on an August morning, just after sunrise but before the heat of day had burned off the morning fog. Two field lights were mysteriously shining brightly through the grey dawn and it looked remarkably as it had years ago, ready for Friday night football.

A modern-day scoreboard showing no score stood in the distance. The playing field was no longer lined with yardage markers but has been reasonably maintained. Goal posts were gone, as was the old concession stand where we bought hamburgers, hot dogs, peanuts, candy bars, and cokes. The adults bought coffee on cool nights, all this well before Starbucks and this new-day coffee craze. Even if we had asked, I doubt they would have served us youngsters' coffee back then. "Stunts your growth" might've been the reply.

Also missing were the short posts and wire cables running down each sideline that kept spectators off the playing field, except that on this field, and I suspect on others, a few old timers sat inside the cable near the thirty-yard line. These gents offered suggestions and health tips to the uniformed officials, such as, "Watch number sixty-five; he is holding every play," or "Off sides, are you blind?" and "They sell glasses at Woolworths." Occasionally, a four-letter word was thrown in to emphasize their point.

A "track" that hadn't been there in the past circled the entire perimeter; I assume it was built for folks to walk or jog around for exercise, but in my youth, I knew of no one who jogged and few who walked on tracks. Folks worked full days back then; rocking chairs and porch sitting were all the rage late in the day. The frequent waves at passersby completed an evening workout.

I walked to where I thought was midway, the fifty-yard line. I did a slow 360 degree turn to take it all in. My eyes and thoughts were drawn to the northwest corner of this oddly rectangular shaped piece of land and to where the baseball field had been. A volunteer pine ten feet high was growing in the spot where the pitcher's mound had been. Beyond that had been a home plate, and beyond that was a backstop constructed of wood planks and chicken wire. This protected the fans from errant pitches thrown by boys dreaming of being the next Whitney Ford or Sandy Koufax. If you don't know who these are, google their names, or trust me when I say boys dreamed of being them when they weren't dreaming of Julie Christie or Natalie Wood.

A six-foot red clay bank, formed when the field was leveled, stood behind the stands. It was perfect for "King of the Hill," a boy's game with the object to stay on top while the competitors attempt to push you off. It also provided hard clay dirt clods for ammo when the games were less organized and without mature guidance.

Our school for which these fields were built was the smallest of the small. We could barely field enough players for a football team. Winning seasons were hard to come by, but my senior year was truly a glorious one in those glory days of our youth. The mighty Wadley Dragons, supported by fans and cheerleaders alike with choruses of "Push em back, push em back, Way back!" and "Block that kick, block that kick!" went undefeated until we lost in a region playoff to a powerhouse that went on to win the state title.

I would like to write that I scored a winning touchdown or made a game saving tackle that year, but if I did it would be a lie. My area of expertise was in procurement for the team, well actually procurement for a couple of team members. We three were rascals, and wins were cause for celebration. While the two friends faced big, fast, and mean players on the field, I had the task of facing grown men selling beer and not returning empty handed. I was underage but had enough gumption to walk in an establishment and ask calmly for the required beverages.

The scheme worked well until one Friday night I came face to face with the owner of the establishment and the father of a classmate. Of course, he knew me and my age and my parents very well. My gumption was about to high tail it out the door I had just come in: busted. All he said was, "Allen, what can I do for you?"

Scared to death, shaking in my boots, I managed to say "Three quarts of PBR."

He smiled, reached in the cooler, pulled out the beer, sacked it in brown paper bags and set it on the counter. "That'll be $2.75. You boys stay out of trouble tonight."

"Yes sir."

I gathered up the bags and left thankful for my good fortune. It might have been easier facing a big ol' mean linebacker.

Those fields I visited on that August morning are part of me and of my glory days, as were the games played and the parents who provided for us, including those who told us to stay out of trouble and the ones that allowed the years to happen.

There is something special about that time that you don't forget. Years made up of things that happened on the playing fields and elsewhere become clearer if you go back for a visit. I relived a few of mine that morning.

It was glorious.

A Man Remembered

A twenty by twenty-foot square piece of Georgia red clay was my destination on a recent beautiful spring morning. This small parcel of land is bordered by a waist-high iron fence made in an ornate hairpin and picket style, all of it rusted and discolored though largely intact. A swinging gate of the same stood frozen open, seemingly an invitation to come in. Words indicating the manufacturer and date "Rogers Fence Company, Springfield OH, Nov 22, 1881," ran across the middle of the gate, near the top in larger bolder text, the name "Gary." I had come to visit Winder Gary, specifically. It had been fifty years and I owed him a visit. I had admired this man. Among other things, cemeteries give rise to our memories.

This solemn place had two rows of flat concrete slabs, four per row and each three feet by seven feet, markers for eight souls, gone. The first one read Winder Gary, Aug. 5,1882 – Oct. 24,1966. Winder Gary doesn't roll of my tongue comfortably. He will forever be Mr. Gary to me and, even though I only knew him as a 70-year-old man, he didn't live as one. On his visits to the farm he took my sisters and me swimming.

Saturday mornings just after daylight, he would arrive at our home in his car, always a new Buick, and take us to a local swimming pool. Mama came along with fried chicken, potato salad, deviled eggs, sandwiches, and gallons of iced tea. Mr. Gary paid for our swimming, bought us co-colas and Zero bars as treats. He swam with us and kept up despite his age. The swimming would go on all day, and only when the sun was going down, the water began to turn cold and our skin looked like prunes did we leave. We may have served as surrogate children, as he had none of his own. That he took the time and trouble to treat us four kids to a full day of enjoyment spoke to the kind of man he was.

He was a graduate of Georgia Tech, a mechanical engineer and lived in Seneca, S.C. He had made a good living in the textile industry, when it was viable, with factories dotting small towns across the Southeast. He visited because he owned the land Dad farmed and the house we lived in until Dad bought it all.

Dad and I visited Mr. Gary in Seneca when I was a young boy and I am not sure why I was along. Maybe Mama wanted me out of her hair for a day, and I can't say I blame her for that. The men discussed business I was not privy to. Perhaps it was when Dad bought the place and they were working out the terms. At his home that evening, shrimp cocktails were served and I thought it to be the best thing I have ever eaten, in fact, so good that I asked for seconds. The two men smiled, then explained it didn't work that way as it was an appetizer. Since my parents had instructed me over and over not to ask so many questions and to accept the answers, I did exactly that, but it didn't stop me from wanting more shrimp, which is still my favorite food, not counting in season home-grown tomatoes.

The last trip I made to Seneca was after Mr. Gary's death. He had been thoughtful and left some beautiful furniture to my Mama. I went along to help with the loading. Mr. Gary was gone and there were no shrimp. The furniture, always cherished by my mama, remains in the family to this day.

Standing there looking over the graves with a beautiful blue sky above, I made note of names and dates. Six were easy. Resting next to Mr. Gary was his wife Lola C. Gary, born 1898. One was marked as Mother, born 1862, and two as Father, born 1821 and 1861, respectively. I think the older one, though I can't be certain, was his grandfather. Finally, a Sallie A. Gary born in 1804 was the first of these to pass on in 1887. The cemetery is that old. The remaining two were sadly blank and left me wondering why. Of the sadness found in a cemetery, an unnamed grave is the poorest testament to a human soul. The worst of us deserve more. We live a life much too short, do some good, and are gone.

When the time comes for each of us, tears are shed, memories told, and a marker laid. There is no way of knowing the future with any certainty, but I do know my time will come. Years may go by, but I hope one day someone thinks of me and decides to visit. Words wouldn't be necessary, but a heartfelt "Hello Allen, I remember when...." wouldn't hurt.

My Two Hearts

The human heart is incredible. It beats as an involuntary action. It beats without a thought from us. It beats when you sleep. It beats when you dream. (Mine beats faster when I dream of Playboy Playmate Miss May 1966.) It beats on an average of 80 times a minute. 4,800 times an hour. 115,200 times a day. 42,048,000 times a year. And for me, a man of seventy, mine has continuously and without failure done this two billion, six hundred ninety-one million, seventy-two thousand times: that's 2,691,072,000. It is a miracle of nature. I have no understanding of how this works, nor am I curious as to why it does. But it does. I will leave those questions to the doctors and the scientists. Doctors are well aware of the heart's importance. Visit one for a hangnail and they will check your heart. In fact, they walk around with a stethoscope close at hand should the need arise. Apparently, it does and often. For me, due either to good genes or just plain old good luck, the checkups have gone well, and this despite many years of a less than healthy heart lifestyle. Others have not been as fortunate.

We learn from a very young age exactly where our heart is. As children we "cross" our heart with a finger, then proclaim, "Cross my heart and hope to die," declaring our commitment to a stated promise. Children don't realize what the real-life consequences could be of such a statement, but I don't question their sincerity. As we grow older, we learn to place our right palm on the heart when pledging allegiance to our country. Young boys who are becoming men learn to remove their hats and place it over the heart during solemn moments, such as prayer. This vital organ, about the size of a fist, is easily found, if not by your heart beat, then by a life of learned experiences. This continuous-working heart, this miracle, gives us life, but it does not give our lives meaning. Our other heart does that.

That one is pesky, the one that won't leave you alone. This other heart of mine has caused me an untold amount of grief. Because of it, I have lost sleep, appetite, and occasionally the use of my brain. This heart has the unique ability to kick the brain's ass. Please, pardon my heart-felt profanity. It's akin to having a psychotic bipolar friend with you 24/7. It's a mess. Stuff happens. Loss of love and of loved ones is big. The cruelty of humanity is another. When bad things happen, your brain will tell you, "It's hard, it will be tough, but you can get through this," and for a brief moment you believe. But this heart of yours cannot leave well enough alone and sends an urgent message to your tear ducts, "Full speed ahead." This heart ends up being bruised, battered, beat up, and sometimes broken, assuming you have the required number of tears behind you. Not from a necessarily tragic life, it often comes from just living an everyday ordinary one. Amazingly, despite all the trials and tribulations, this heart heals itself eventually, or at least heals enough to carry on with manageable sadness. Occasionally, stories are told of gentle, but unfortunate, folks who have died of a broken one.

These two hearts are inside every human. For evidence, spend some time with two-year olds. Watch them play; listen to their laughter. Laughter comes from this heart, as do tears. One needs to be on guard and mindful, for when terrible, tragic things happen, loss of this heart is possible. Most tragic is the life of one called "hard-hearted" or "cold-hearted" or, even worse, "heartless."

Just recently the doctor said my beating heart is doing just fine. That's good news, for I have life yet to live. However, I don't want to live it with just a beating heart. The other one may be pesky and troublesome at times, but I am pretty sure you can't properly appreciate a child's happiness, view a beautiful morning sunrise, or thoroughly enjoy your pretty wife's kiss without it.

And so, here's to you, and to the health of your two hearts on life's journey.

8

Jake

Ike, the inspiration for "Jake" stories.

Varmints

Southwest Florida was the home of my youth and was as far south as you could go without walking into Gulf of Mexico. It was swampland filled with huge numbers of nasty varmints. Men called it the Everglades (large fields of grass). They dug canals to drain off the water in an effort to make it habitable. Still it was a harsh region. I had witnessed the young being bitten by poisonous snakes or worse, snatched away by alligators never to be seen again. I was one of the lucky ones.

I lived on a citrus farm with James Powell, a young man with big ideas but with no love for the land nor of the crops he grew. Some days he bounced from task to task, starting many but finishing none. My duty was to follow him, so I did, without question.

James spied the visitor right after I did and walked toward the gate. I looked to see a man walking up the lane to the farm. Visitors were scarce, as the farm was over a canal bridge, right on a dirt road for two miles, then left and at the end of an unmarked sandy trail. The farm perimeter was completely fenced although there were no livestock to be kept in. It was there solely to keep folks like this stranger out.

James' greeting was to the point. "What can I do for you?"

The visitor replied, "Good morning. I was told you might be looking for help."

"I don't know where you got that; I keep my business to myself," James snarled.

"Truth is, there was no mention of a job, but I did hear there was a farm out here and hoped there might be work and a place to stay."

"I have a tenant house and lots of work that needs to be done," James replied. "How can you help me?"

"Well sir, I have a natural feel for all things green and growing and am a decent enough mechanic when called on."

James looked the man over and thought he might do. He hadn't had any help since he had run off the last one, weeks ago. "Guess I could use a man to help with all the citrus and equipment. What you say to a hundred a week and a place to stay?"

The visitor stuck a strong right hand across the top of the gate between them and says, "I'd be mighty appreciative, Mr...?"

James didn't offer his hand in return, instead opened the gate and pointed at me, "This here is Jake; my name is James Powell. Come on in and close the gate TIGHT behind you."

We three walked from the main house through orchards of navel oranges and key limes before coming to the tenant house, a small wood-sided building with a tin roof and a screened porch. The porch was shaded and provided a cool respite from the Florida sun. On the walk I smelled no fear nor hate on this unknown visitor. Rather I took an immediate liking to him and wagged my tail to show my pleasure.

James looked to the new man: "Make yourself at home. I got some errands to run but will be back this evening and we can discuss what needs to be done tomorrow. We will do the same each and every evening."

"Thank you, sir, I am happy to be of service. My name is Ray Alexander."

James walked off without replying; he could not care less what the man's name was. I followed along.

Every night I was fed outside at the main house and left alone, James inside counting his pennies. One evening bored and lonely, I trotted over to the tenant house and found Ray on the porch, drinking beer and rolling smokes. He greeted me: "How you doing, Jake?" I wagged my tail in response. He was kind and spoke from his heart. In a couple of hours, he retired for the night and I walked back to the main house. It wasn't long before I began to spend nights on the back porch of the tenant house with my new-found friend inside.

Early one morning James caught me sleeping at the tenant house and yelled, "JAKE, YOU GET ON BACK TO THE HOUSE!"

I jumped up and started off, then stopped. James was pounding on the door to wake Ray. As quick as Ray opened the door, James lit into him, yelling, "RAY, YOU BEEN FEEDING MY DOG?"

"No sir."

"WELL, WHY IS HE STAYING HERE AT NIGHT WHEN HE OUGHT TO BE AT THE MAIN HOUSE?"

"I don't know."

"I WON'T HAVE YOU TAKING MY DOG, YOU HEAR ME? YOU MAKE DAMN SURE HE IS AT MY PLACE EVERY NIGHT!"

"Yes sir."

James then headed back toward the main house, grabbing me by the collar and pulling me along.

That evening I followed James over to the tenant house, assuming they would discuss the next day's work as always. On the back porch sat Ray, relaxing in a chair, a packed knapsack at his side. James, seeing the knapsack, pointed it out and asked, "What's that about?"

"Well sir, you been good enough to me, but there are a couple hours of daylight left and I must be on my way."

"Now Ray, ain't no reason to run off like that."

"Yes sir, I need to go. Going to miss old Jake for sure, but little else on this varmint-ridden place."

He reached for the top of my head, scratched behind my ears and said, "So long my friend, you are fine company. Of all the things here, you are the only one I will miss."

He walked into the lime orchard headed toward the gate and disappeared. I looked up at James' scowling face and smelled his hate. I turned and took off after Ray. He was right. Snakes, gators, and a hard man, too many varmints lived in this place.

Jake and the Old Man

Abe had an affinity for animals including even the smallest, most destructive insects. He rarely spoke of animals with harsh words. A neighbor stopped by one day, complaining and grumbling about the bugs in his bean patch. He replied to the neighbor:

"You know everyone of God's creatures got to eat and find its way in this world. I don't have any animosity toward those bugs. On the other hand, I do what I have to do to raise a mess of beans for my wife and me."

The old man loved cows, chickens, and cats. He made sure all the animals were well fed and watered daily. The cows provided food and income. The chickens and cats were there primarily for his entertainment, though he would never admit this fact. He loved to hear the roosters crowing and kept hens so the roosters would have something to crow about. The cats helped by lowering the rodent population, but mostly he loved their curious nature. The cat population went up and down but there always seemed to be at least a dozen roaming the barns and small sheds. There was a Gracie, a Honey, and a Blackie. Sometimes he named one after men in the news, Roosevelt being one of his favorites. He fed them on the back porch twice a day and was the only one who could pet them. The cats enjoyed a peaceful existence since he owned no dog. He thought dogs needy and troublesome with their barking and chasing although he had no specific animosity toward the creatures.

Early one morning while loosening the oil drain plug under his tractor, he felt a presence and looked to see at his feet a black dog sitting on its haunches, tongue hanging out as if it were tired and thirsty. With his attention diverted, the drain plug came loose and dropped to the grass. The oil missed the bucket he'd meant to catch it, puddling on the ground. It streamed under his back and soaked his work shirt. In disgust, he slid out from under the tractor, stood up soaked in motor oil, and glared at the dog.

Aggravated, he spoke to the animal, "I am going to blame you for this, but I don't think the old woman is going to be happy with either of us. Come on," he said, pointing at the back door; "we got some explaining to do."

The man turned and headed toward the house. Halfway there he glanced back to check on the new-found mutt and discovered that the dog, as if he understood, was following close behind.

Near the backdoor was a spigot, under which lay an old hubcap that caught the excess water and served as a watering dish for the cats and chickens. As they walked by, the dog stopped. The man looked back and grumbled at the dog, "All right I guess you are thirsty. Get a drink; I'll face the woman on my own. If she fusses too much, I'll send her out here to meet you."

The man, clearly displaying his annoyance with the morning's developments, plodded on to the back steps and went inside. The dog's ears raised each time he heard loud voices from the house, his eyes fixed on the screen door.

A few minutes later the man came back out wearing a clean shirt and carrying an old fry pan full of table scraps. He spoke to the dog, "You are a fine-looking animal, but it appears you been traveling for a day or two."

He sat the pan down near the dog and said, "Eat up! Looks like I am in the dog house and may need your help to get out. We will figure that out, but first I'll clean up the mess you and I made under the tractor."

The dog sheepishly looked up at the man and watched him walk away before attacking the table scraps.

The old man had cleaned up the mess and begun to pour new oil in the tractor when the dog came over with a look of contentment and sat down. Pleased with the animal's behavior he said, "I know all my neighbors and their dogs, and I have never seen you. Will have to check around and see if I can find your home. In the meantime, need to call you something. What's your name?"

The dog tilted his head sideways.

"Well then, I always liked the name Jake. What do you think about that?"

The old man paused in the conversation as if to give the dog a chance to answer. The dog appeared to smile. "OK, since you have no objection, Jake it is."

Finishing the cleanup, he wiped his brow and looked up at the sun, "Jake, it's about lunch time. You just ate but I haven't, and I am hungry. I am going to see what she has. Don't bother nothing that ain't bothering you and, if you do that, we will get along just fine."

The dog looked at the man as if in agreement.

Putting his hand tools away, the farmer walked towards the house, with the dog following by his side. Halfway there, Jake stopped by the water spigot where the empty fry pan lay. Smiling, Abe turned, and said, "You are smart, easygoing and friendly enough, and I haven't heard you bark once. There is something special about you, ole boy." Jake wagged his tail for the first time and lay down. The old man went on in to make amends and see what was for lunch. He hadn't felt this good in a long time; though he might not admit it yet to himself or to the woman, he knew it was because of the dog.

Jake's New Home

Abe woke at dawn, same as every other morning. There was clock on the night stand but he had little use for it. His work day was determined by what needed to be done, but it always started early. Mostly it was tending to the cows, his hired hand did the fieldwork. Even when the rest of the country went to or from Daylight Savings time, his clock never changed. It was only Sunday mornings he needed to pay particular attention to time because Ida wanted them in church on time.

This was not a Sunday and the old woman was already up; per their ritual she rose to prepare breakfast as soon as she heard him stirring. He made his way to the bathroom where he washed and shaved. He always shaved. He believed it put a fresh start on a new day. He then made his way to the kitchen where his wife was busy with her work. She sat a steaming cup of black coffee in front of him as soon as he sat down. His morning thoughts had been about the dog and he wondered if he was still around. As if she knew what he was thinking, she said, "The food is ready for the cats and the dog."

He looked and saw two pans of prepared food, when usually there was only one. "OK, I will go feed them."

When he opened the back door, the cats were there waiting and meowing as if they were starving to death. As it was what they always did, he smiled. Over the years he had grown fond of this behavior. He sat the pan of food down. "Alright now y'all eat and hush up."

Sure that the cats were settled, he looked for signs of the dog. There were none. He walked to the back of the porch and looked out across the yard toward the barns. Nothing. "Jake!" he called out. Nothing. "Jake! Jake!" he called again. A blur of black came running and bounded up on the porch to greet him. The cats scattered. This caused the old man to laugh and say, "Glad to see you, old boy, but the cats ain't. I better feed you out in the yard, but don't let it bother you, those old cats don't like nobody but me."

Together they walked, man and dog across the yard to the water spigot. There he sat the pan of food for Jake down. Unlike the cats, Jake didn't go right to eating, rather he sidled up next to Abe's pants leg as if to say thanks. Abe reached down and stroked Jake's head, the first time he had touched the dog. Jake stood there calmly looking up at him. Abe immediately felt a place in him filled, a place that had been empty. He smiled and said, "Go ahead and eat."

Jake did as he was told, and his new master turned and walked back to the house.

Inside he announced, "He is still here."

Ida replied, "I guess you have a new friend and another mouth to feed."

Abe said, "I don't know, he might be a neighbor's dog. Later I will ride over to check with some of them."

He sat down at the kitchen table and she brought over his breakfast. After a few minutes he turned to her and said, "Ida, is there anything we need?"

She thought for a minute and replied, "Well, if you're going to town, I could use some buttermilk." He smiled at her reply. "I didn't mean it like that. The dog got me to thinking. Are our lives full?"

"Abe, we have everything we need, we have a good home and we have each other, but if you want to buy something, you can buy me a new stove. This one is about as old as you."

He smiled but said nothing. She went on, "I'm just kidding you. We don't need a new stove; this one cooks just fine, but I do need some buttermilk."

Later that day he drove into town to the grocery store where he bought a quart of buttermilk and bag of dog food. He also bought an expensive box of chocolate candy for his wife. She truly loved chocolate. Driving home, he considered going by the neighbors to ask about a missing black dog but his heart wasn't in it. Another time, another day would be soon enough.

Jake Goes to Town

As Abe finished his meal, he reached for the sweet tea and poured himself a full glass. His wife Ida knew this meant he wanted to sit and talk a spell. She was glad for these times for he wasn't much of a talker. "I am going into town this afternoon to the cemetery."

This was something he did from time to time; he called it cleaning the family plot. He did some of that, but she and he both knew it was more. "I can go and help," she offered.

"Naw, but you will need to get some new flowers for it in a couple of weeks."

After years of marriage, their roles were defined.

She decided to tease him and said, "You could go by the florist and pick out something."

He said, "What do I know about picking out flowers?"

She replied, "What if I was gone, what would you do then?"

"Ida, I suppose Mrs. Chatham down at the florist shop could help me with flowers, but if you were gone, I would surely miss your cornbread and sweet tea."

"Abe, you know I was just kidding, where you think I am going?"

"Never can tell, you might run off with a traveling salesman." She laughed and replied, 'Ain't no traveling salesman looking for an old biddie like me."

"Shucks, Ida, don't make us old. You still a spring chick, same as the one I courted all those years back."

She had known when she first met him that he wasn't the most romantic of men, but she loved him all the same and said, "You better get on about your business before I take a switch to you."

He smiled and said, "Thank you ma'am for the warning. By the way, I'm gonna take Jake with me." Though she didn't respond, she was pleased he might have a new friend.

At the tool shed, Abe picked up a foot tub. In it were some rags, a bar of the soap, a gallon jug of water, and an old bristle brush. He found Jake laying under the mimosa tree in the backyard napping. "Jake, you want to go to town?" Jake's ears perked up. Abe wasn't sure, but it seemed this dog understood everything he said. Jake had never been to town. The old man lowered the truck tailgate and Jake sailed in. He usually ran behind the truck on the farm but he had quickly learned when the man lowered the tailgate it was an invitation. Abe set the tub in the back with Jake, closed the tailgate and off they went.

It was a mild winter day and a short drive to the cemetery. He parked, got out, let the tailgate down for Jake, grabbed the foot tub and walked over to the family plot. Jake walked with him and stopped by his side. His father, his mother, and his older sister were laid to rest there. He thought back to the time when they were still alive, when he was younger. It felt good to remember. Jake lay quietly nearby as if he understood the need for respect and reverence.

Not a man who stood idle for long, he began with his favorite task. With the brush, soap, and water from the jug, he began scrubbing the engravings, the names and dates. He couldn't remember when he had started doing this but it felt good. He thought of it as brushing their teeth, a silly thought for a man his age he told himself, but it reminded him of their smiles, of the good times they had shared as a family. When he finished with the engravings, he wiped the granite monuments of excess water and any remaining soil. Completing all he intended to do that day, he stepped back to admire his work and for some last thoughts. He wondered about the way of the world, how life is short, and if there couldn't be a better way. He looked to Jake and said, "Jake, what do you make of this life?" Jake looked bewildered by the question. The old man smiled at Jake's expression and said, "Yes sir, I reckon that's a deep question. Maybe I will ask Ida."

Usually the old man went directly home after the visit to the cemetery, but this day he drove on into town and parked in front of Wilcher's grocery store. He got out, looked to Jake and said, "You stay right here, I need to pick up something and will be right back."

Jake looked agreeable. The old man walked in and found Mr. Wilcher, "Sam, I need something for Ida." Sam says, "I got lard on sale, or maybe she would like five pounds of cornmeal?"

"Naw Sam, I mean something more personal, something women folk like."

"I don't know Abe, we don't carry woman doodads, but we got some real nice strawberries in this morning."

"That's a good idea Sam, she likes strawberries and she might make a pie."

Standing, waiting for Sam to bring the strawberries, he saw through the glass front of Wilcher's store two towheaded children standing by his truck. They were young and could barely reach up high enough to stroke Jake's head even when he had lowered his head over the side to assist them. Sam came back with the strawberries and the old man said, "Much obliged Sam, all right if we settle up at the end of the month?"

Sam nodded his head in approval and the old man walked out.

The children saw him coming and asked, "Mister Abe, is this your dog?"

"He is, his name is Jake."

"How did he get so black? We never seen one this black."

"Well, he showed up at my farm early one morning from traveling all night. I reckon the black of the night just stuck to him."

"We sure would like to play with him sometime. Can we?"

"Sure you can, go ask your mama if she will bring you out to my place, you can stay as long as you want. Jake will be glad to see you."

"Let's go ask mama!" one of them half-shouted and they took off lickety-split.

Abe stood by the side of the truck stroking Jake's head and was suddenly content with the world. He looked at Jake and said, "Well now, Jake, there you have it. Us folks get old, we retire, we pass on, and the children take our place. I guess it's alright. I will ask Ida about it when I give her the strawberries; she likes to talk anyway."

As It Should Be

The piercing sound woke Jake. It was a man-made, screaming noise dying away in the distance as the seconds ticked by. It brought pain to his sensitive canine ears. He was accustomed to being roused by the comforting voice of the man calling, "Jake, Jake." To Jake those words meant, "Wake up, breakfast is ready."

His master had learned when Jake was a pup that he was a sleepy head, always teasing the dog for being slow to rise.

"Me and the chickens have already done a half day's work."

or

"If you don't get up, the cat's going to have at your breakfast."

or

"You so lazy I am going to have to dock your pay."

The teasing didn't bother Jake; he heard heart in the words and always wagged his tail, as if he shared a laugh at the teasing.

Despite the obnoxious sound that had stirred him, he did as he had always done in anticipation of a new day. He gathered himself up and ran fast as his long, muscular legs would carry him to the back steps of the farm house. Sliding to a stop, he immediately felt unsure and confused; the human he lived for was not there, nor was there any breakfast. Once an impatient young dog, he had learned patience from the man and lay down in the cool green grass, wet from the morning dew, waiting. Although it seemed an eternity to Jake, in a few minutes the back door opened. He jumped to his feet and began wagging his tail only to be further bewildered when the woman walked out carrying two pans of food. She sat one down for the meowing cats and walked toward him with the other. Her movement was awkward, tedious as if she carried the world's burdens. Although they hadn't been close, Jake nuzzled her hand in affection with his wet nose as she set the round pan of food on the top step.

With a sigh, she said, "You're a good boy, Jake, but things are bad. Abe woke feeling poorly. I called the ambulance and they have taken him to the hospital. It was the hardest thing I have ever done, letting him go in that thing alone."

She went quiet, then said, "He insisted I look after you and the cats. He said the chickens can look after themselves. He shouldn't be in that place by himself, Jake. Sadie Mae is coming to pick me up because I hate driving his raggedy old truck. Mr. Turner is coming by to check on the cows. Thank the Lord for good neighbors."

She looked directly at him and with a soft, trembling voice said, "It doesn't look good Jake; it doesn't look good at all. I can't live without Abe. What would we do?"

Jake had yet to take a bite as he let her finish talking. When she finally turned and walked toward the back door, he dug in, finishing his meal in seconds. Confused by the morning events, he still expected the man to come out and the two of them, as they always did, go feed the cows. It was eerily quiet. Jake couldn't figure it, so he walked over and lay down by the man's truck. Minutes later he heard a car coming up the dirt road. He sat up on his front legs to see the woman come out and get in the car, then drive away, leaving him alone with the aggravating cats and the noisy chickens.

He fell asleep waiting and dreamed. He dreamed running alongside the truck on the way to the silo to feed the cows. He dreamed of the man swerving at him playfully, running him in the ditch with a tumble, and his muscular body and strong legs quickly springing him upright, out of the ditch and back on the road. He dreamed of the man's smile when he caught back up, the kind only true friends share--in this case a young dog and a man whose youth had left him, though not entirely. Jake lived for these moments.

The dream woke him, and he began to search for the man. He wandered to the back door and scratched it with his paw; there was no sound but his own whimper. He wandered to the workshop; he smelled the tools the man used and he caught the man's scent. It was an old scent that was comforting to the confused canine. He wandered back to the truck and went to sleep again. Late in the day he heard a car, saw it pull up, the woman get out and go inside. Soon she called from the back porch with his supper and he went running. "Here you go, Jake, you hungry? Abe is not coming home today; he is terribly sick. He couldn't talk much but told me to go home and to be sure to feed you. Goodnight, Jake."

Without another word she turned and walked in the house. She wasn't an uncaring person toward the dog or the cats or the chickens. It was the circumstance. This went on for days and days. She would feed him in the morning, leave with her friend, be gone all day, and feed him again just before dark when she returned.

And then one evening just before dusk, she returned and, as Jake watched, the man was slowly helped out of the car. In a flash Jake ran towards him, overcome with joy.

The man spoke weakly, "Calm down, Jake, I am glad to see you, too. Ida, get me over to the stoop, I want to talk to him."

With the woman's help he sat down gently on the top step; Jake sat down at his side. The old man draped his arm across the dog and, scratching him behind the ears, said, "Jake, my old heart was worn out. After the Doctor patched it up, I did a lot of sleeping. One day I dreamed we were headed to feed the cows and I run you in the ditch with the truck, playful like. You come out of the ditch like a dog afire and caught back up. This dream truly warmed my old heart. I figure the only time I had more fun was one evening courting this old woman Ida here on her daddy's porch. We were sitting in his swing and I stole me a kiss, the sweetest one I ever had."

The man's warm words comforted both dog and woman. The man's eyes spoke love for both, his smile weak but wide from thoughts of the past. Ida's did, too. Jake wagged his tail briskly. All his world was right again, as it should be.

A Time Remembered

The old man woke from a deep sleep and from a dream of times gone by, his blue eyes moist with tears, his worn-out heart saddened. The pain was gone but he was tired. He tried to remember how long he had been tired, but his mind was jumbled. He missed his wife. "I must have slept through her visits," the memory of her passing gone. Days and nights ran together. Then another memory flashed through his mind and for a brief moment he was as happy as he had ever been. He grinned and mumbled to himself, "My old dog used to sleep all the time, too."

After a few minutes came a soft knock at the door and a woman's voice, "May we come in?"

He grunted "Aw' right" and in walked a pretty woman he couldn't place, and a young girl, whom he guessed was four or five. Ages of children were hard for him. It didn't matter; he smiled because of her presence. The woman spoke, "I came to visit and brought my granddaughter along. This is Jodi.

He didn't reply. She had seen him like this, so she went on, "How are you feeling?"

"I'm aw' right, but the doctors won't let me go home. Makes me mad, but what can I do? Anyway, just before you came, I had a memory. Would y'all like to hear about it?"

The woman said, "That would be nice."

He looked to the young child, "Jodi, do you have a dog?"

Without uttering a sound, she timidly shook her head from side to side.

The old man began, "I had the best dog when I was a young fella. I guess it was somewhere around 1974. His name was Jake and he was a Labrador retriever, black as the night. At the time I was farming with my father, and late that summer dad hired a man to clear out a small thicket of trees so we would have more land to work."

He continued, "Jodi, do you know what a bulldozer is?"

She shook her head side to side again but this time with more assurance.

"It's a big yellow machine that can push up trees. The man came to the farm and went to work. He pushed all the trees on that piece of ground into a huge pile. In the fall in cooler weather, the wood would've dried, we could set it on fire to burn it up. That would give us another acre to grow corn or winter wheat."

His mind, clearer now from telling the story, continued, "The time came and my father thought it a good day to burn. It was cold and cloudy; a warm fire from the dried pile of trees would be welcome. I loaded the tools needed in the back of the truck and in jumped Jake. There were times dad didn't want the dog along, but he nodded his head in approval and I slammed the tailgate shut. Our task was to walk the cleared land, pick up branches and small pieces the dozer had missed, and burn them with the trees the dozer had pushed together earlier that year. When Dad tossed the first piece at the pile, old Jake reacted just the way a retriever is supposed to react. He took off after the stick, dove in, brought it back and dropped it at our feet. I did the same and Jake did the same again. Dad smiled and I laughed. We tossed a few more and Ol'Jake brought 'em back. We were getting nowhere fast. I half expected dad to scold the dog, but he was a man who appreciated the work of men and beasts, so said to me, "Jake is just doing what he was born to do."

We tried both of us throwing a piece at the same time. As usual, Jake retrieved one, which made him happy, and left one, which made us happy. I surely enjoyed that day working with my father and Jake.

The man's mind working well from the memory, he went on. "It's funny when you get near the end, the things that stand out.

Odd to be thinking of a dog long gone. I suppose I didn't appreciate my time with him enough. Don't believe there is a thing in this world I would rather do right this minute, but to throw a stick and see him get after it."

The old man having finished his story looked to his visitors and said after a moment, "I appreciate y'all coming. Jodi, did you like the story?"

She grinned a wide, bright grin that only the very young possess, and nodded her head up and down in affirmation.

"Well, come again and I will tell you how Jake learned about a cow's business end the hard way. But don't worry, it didn't hurt him much."

And with that the woman rose, bent over him and kissed him on the cheek.

"Aw shucks, my daughter used to do that."

"I know, Dad.

The puzzled look in the old man eyes brought tears to his daughter's. A soft spoken "We love you" was all she could manage. Feeling there was nothing further to be gained on this visit, she took the young child's hand, bid goodbye and started out. The old man watched as they left hand in hand and felt life would be good to them. They seemed nice. Truth is, he needed them to go; he was tired and wanted to sleep. He closed his eyes and, in his mind, he saw a black dog, dark as the night, chasing after a stick thrown across the Georgia sky. The image warmed his heart and he smiled of a life well lived as he joined his stick-chasing dog for eternity.

9

Change

Dad

Death of the Family Farm

Every mile or so were white wooden or red brick houses surrounded by weathered barns with tin roofs and farm equipment of every description, kids, dogs, and chickens running free. During the fifties and sixties, such small farms dotted rural America and were thriving. In the seventies family farms started dying. Even more importantly, a lifestyle faded away like wilting crops.

In 1973 I came back to our family farm after spending five years in Athens going to school. Things hadn't changed much. You planted a crop in the spring and harvested it in the fall. Prices for crops, prices for equipment, and prices for fuel had remained relatively the same since the early fifties. A good farmer could make a living and raise a family on a modest hard-earned income. Life was good. All of that changed with the oil embargo and I was there to see it.

"In response to the US aid to Israel, on October 16, 1973, OPEC announced a decision to raise the posted price of oil by 70%, to $5.11 a barrel. The following day, oil ministers agreed to the embargo, a cut in production by five percent from September's output, and to continue to cut production over time in five percent increments until their economic and political objectives were met."

The following spring the price of oil went from $3 a barrel to $12, along with it, the price of gasoline and diesel fuel. If you are old enough, you may remember gas shortages and long lines at gas stations. You may remember odd even days, which meant if your car tag ended with an odd number you could buy gas on an odd numbered day, even number, even numbered days. Farming is a petroleum-based business, from the fuel required to operate equipment to fertilizer which requires large amounts of oil for its production. With the increase in oil, cost of production for farmers rose dramatically without a similar rise in market prices for the crops grown, thus the beginning of the end for many family farms.

During this same time a land boom began. The average price for farmland in our area went from three hundred to one thousand dollars per acre. A short-term blessing, a long-term death. It meant a farmer could borrow more money to keep his operation going, but at the same time increase his debt, which meant he would need more income to service this debit. The increase in farm income didn't happen. Family farms were dying.

Over the years that I farmed with dad, we discussed the things to plant each spring, the different ways we could make a profitable crop, assuming good weather. Unfortunately, the weather turned and there were frequent droughts. Adding to our misery, markets remained stagnant and costs kept rising. In the late seventies I decided to throw in the towel, I was a young man and wanted a different future. I sat down with dad and told him I wanted to sell out. He said to me, "You're doing the right thing."

I asked, "This is a tough business; how have you done so well over the years?"

His reply: "It was different when I got started, but times change, things change. If I was a younger man…," his voice trailed off.

When I travel those country roads, I see homes where I once knew the family who lived there. The folks are gone, moved on, their small farm swallowed up by a larger operation or planted in pine trees. I see the towns, formerly dependent on small farmers, now stagnant, some dying. In a span of forty years, an industry changed completely and dramatically impacted rural America.

Now I am hopeful, for I am beginning to see signs of life in those ashes--small niche farming, inventive retail, organic produce, and farm to table marketing. Given time, small farming may come back to something like I remember. That is my hope. For in the words of my wise father, "Times change, things change."

True, or maybe they just go in circles.

https://en.wikipedia.org/wiki/1973_oil_crisis

Harvest

I find that memories faded away all too often, now that I am nearing my seventh decade. Memories that were clear yesterday or the day before or last week disappear. Where do they go? I am pleased, however, to be ever aging, the alternative certainly a worse fate. In an ideal world I would still have the recall of the skinny, towheaded schoolboy I once was. I would also have his energy and head of hair.

However, fortune still smiles and a normal everyday happening may at any time send a bolt of lightning made of good memories. My guess is that it jars a synapse in my brain and a remembrance from times faded shines through. That's my idea anyway. I expect there is an authentic scientific explanation for this phenomenon, but frankly I am too old to give a damn. I was struck just so this past week and now am prompted to write of it.

"Allen, we are harvesting corn, come out and drive the combine," the invite went. It has now been forty years since I sat in one of those machines. As I remember it, the driver rides in a cab fixed over the machine's header with hundreds of moving parts underneath and behind, steering down rows of brown stalks, watching corn ears being ripped off the stalks, eaten by the roaring mechanical beast, and spitting the refuse out the rear.

I find a field of corn visually pleasing, green plants first appearing as small sprouts peering out of the earth early spring, growing into knee high ones and then taller than a man in hot summer, uniform lines like a long row of soldiers standing at attention. Given enough water under the Georgia sun, it becomes a magnificent mass of foliage and protein, food for livestock and man alike.

My memory stirred by the invitation to drive, I thought of the times in my youth when I rode a farm machine all day. I remembered Dad coming by mid-afternoons with a Coke in hand. When we weren't up against time, I would shut down the equipment and ride with him to town, stop at the cafe with sweet ice tea for me and he a black coffee. Dead of winter or a summer day of one hundred degrees, didn't matter, he always had black coffee. I was pleased for the reward he provided, if for no other reason than to wash the dust from my throat.

Following up on the invitation and the memory, I stopped and bought cold Cokes for the men I assumed to be helping with the harvest. I had no intention of driving the harvester. Arriving, I found a larger group of men than I had Cokes for, as well as three semis with trailers, and a green John Deere harvester big as a house and three times larger than the machines of my youth. I watched as it crawled through the field eating the corn stalks and filling its hopper with a golden yellow stream of shelled corn, a thing of beauty to a once small-time country farmer. I offered the cokes and apologized for not bringing enough. The men smiled, seemingly pleased for the thought and said so. It turned out their Yeti coolers were well stocked since there wasn't time for a trip to the cafe. Things have changed.

Many of you may not be as thrilled by a corn crop or the harvesting as am I. I hope you at least appreciate corn as the crop that provides you with grits. Probably the most Southern dish of them all, grits, once considered a common dish for breakfast, has now moved into five-star restaurants and is now served as a gourmet meal at dinner. I enjoyed shrimp and grits the other evening and paid twenty-five dollars for it. My father wouldn't believe it. A five-pound bag cost a nickel in his day. Times have most definitely changed.

Old Timer

An "Old timer" is defined as a person with lots of experience or just as an old person. Synonyms are *ancient, elder, golden-ager, oldster, senior,* and *senior citizen*. A good portion of society would now consider me one. What can I say? If the shoe fits. This story is about two old timers: my dad as I remember him, and me, the one I am becoming.

Old Timer is also a brand of pocket knives, and one came in the mail today. It was packaged in a padded manila envelope, 6" X 10" in size. The postage was $3.75. My younger sister Laura was the sender. The knife had been my father's.

To avoid damage during transit, she had wrapped it in soft cotton and placed it in a small cardboard box like those used for jewelry. I doubt the Post Office would have damaged it, but she had done the right thing. It is a priceless remembrance.

I had days earlier emailed and asked if she had any old family pictures of Mom, Dad, us children, the house, barns, anything? She emailed some pictures and wrote this,

"I am going through boxes of Mom and Dad's stuff. Dad's includes his last pair of boots, the American flag that draped his coffin, his dog tag, his pocket knife, high school diploma, first report card from University of Georgia, and military discharge."

She finished with, "Do you want anything?"

Sincere with her offering, I looked the list over, considered the dog tags and flag for a moment and emailed her back.

"I would like the knife."

I thought I needed it. It felt like the right choice.

All the other things I left to her safe keeping for other family members or future generations who one day may want to know more about him.

Called an Old Timer 34OT Middleman, these knives are still sold and are not expensive. An online ad reads:

> This Schrade Middleman is the quintessential pocket knife. The three straight-edged blades are made from high-quality stainless steel and feature three unique blade types: sheepsfoot, spey and clip. In addition to these efficient blades, the knife's 3.31-inch closed length makes it ideal for carrying and using for quick tasks. Experience the craft of Old Timer knives by gripping the comfortable grooves in the handle and maneuvering the compact knife effortlessly. This knife truly lives up to its reputation as one of the most reliable and long-lasting knives on the market.

Stamped in metal on one side of the knife were the capitalized letters "OLD TIMER." Two of the three blades still have a nice edge and cut paper clean, just now. He must have honed it for the last time in 1993, the year of his death, twenty-five years ago. It serves as a tangible, hold-in-your hand, steel reminder of his work.

Over the years I saw him use it to clean his nails and to pick away dirt and grime from a bolt on a planter or disc plow that needed loosening or replacing. I saw him cut open dozens of seed and fertilizer bags. He cut twine from hay bales and rope that tied down a load on his truck.

Known as the Watermelon Man, he determined the perfect ripeness of a melon with a firm thump using his index and middle finger. I watched him over the years check the accuracy of his thump using this knife. When he dragged the shiny blade across the green rind of the melon in question, a perfectly harvested one would burst open. A slight nod indicated all was right with his harvest; a grunt meant otherwise.

Once I heard an old timer remark that if a farmer or farm worker came to work without his knife and handkerchief, he wasn't properly dressed. This knife of Dad's, a memory of a life lived, feels good in my hand and now in my left pants pocket, not too heavy, comfortable. Keys in the right pocket, wallet in back. I took it for a walk to show him my tomatoes, the flowers, the ponds, the dogs and cats. I hope he is proud of this old timer, me. If I just had a handkerchief, I'd be properly dressed.

Southern Fried

Cat head biscuits, fried chicken, turnip greens, pinkeye purple hull peas, fried fish, deviled eggs, macaroni and cheese, peach cobbler, mashed potatoes, lacy cornbread, okra, barbecue, hush puppies, banana pudding, sliced tomatoes, chicken fried steak, pimento cheese, pound cake, butter beans, grits, and sweet tea: we in the South y'all and we eating fine.

Southerners have a thing about food. They believe it fixes everything. With death or sickness neighbors will knock on your door offering fried chicken, baked ham, or a casserole. This obsession is cultural and its roots extend to the Civil War, often called in the South the War of Northern Aggression. War causes shortages of every kind and this one was no exception, especially after General William Tecumseh Sherman's "March to the Sea." What his troops didn't burn, they stole. They left Southerners with nothing and Sherman became the most hated man in Dixie. The conditions of the time were dramatized in the greatest movie ever made, *Gone with the Wind*, when Scarlett took a bite out of a half rotten radish, looked up to the heavens and said, "As God is my witness, I will never be hungry again."

Just as Southerners were getting back on their feet and finally finding some forgiveness for those "damn Yankees," the Depression came along. I didn't live during the Depression despite what some will say about my age, but my father did. When Mama came home from the store complaining about the cost of groceries, Dad would tell her, "Be glad it's plentiful and we have the money to buy it." I try to remember those words and to be thankful for my many blessings. This world is still full of folks not as fortunate.

Living on a farm, my family and I ate well. Dad butchered cows and we ate steak more than most town folks. In the summer months, the garden supplied us with fresh vegetables and Mama put up dozens of cans and jars of vegetables for the winter months. My mother was a very good cook when she had the time and patience for it. When she didn't, when four "young'uns" were under foot, she lost her patience and burned many a dish. Just this morning at breakfast, the waitress serving me apologized and said, "Sorry Allen, the toast is burnt." I replied with a sweet memory and a big grin, "It's OK, that's just the way Mom used to make it."

My favorite Southern cook was Miss Alma Marshall, my maternal grandmother, also known in the family as "Big Mama." She fixed (Yankee readers, "fixed" means cooked.) a smothered fried chicken dish that I would give dollars to enjoy again. On our Sunday afternoon visits she served homemade pound cake with icy cold cokes, the original six and a half ounces bottled in thick emerald green glass. Coke, or "co-colas" as we called them, have gone downhill ever since. Today's plastic bottles or aluminum cans will never provide "co-colas" so cold or so satisfying.

During my twenties, I put my feet under the table of many old-school cooks. My other favorites, Miss Mary and Miss Reba, were mothers of boyhood friends. (Yankee readers, "Miss" is not only for young Misses, but also for Mrs., as with these women. Calling an adult female by her first name preceded with "Miss" was a sign of respect and familiarity. It was Southern and still is today.) Regardless of the meal, their tables would be covered with four or five vegetables, two meats minimum, homemade biscuits or cornbread or both, and all the cold sweet tea you could drink. Your glass never got empty and the offers of another pork chop, another helping of peas were endless. I learned quickly the more you ate, the better pleased they were. I was young with a bottomless pit and happy to oblige. Although additional compliments aren't particularly needed, I must say neither ever served me liver. God bless them.

My eating habits have changed over the years. The bottomless pit is gone, and today in my seventies, I do very well on single servings and a nicely portioned dessert when offered. My thoughts on the therapeutic value of food has changed as well. Neither the variety nor the serving size truly made those home cooked meals memorable; it was and always will be the love Southern women stir in the peas, bake in the cakes, fry in the chicken, and offer freely.

In closing, I will remind you of a scene from the greatest movie ever made and of Scarlett's remark the first time she saw Rhett: "He looks as if... as if he knows what I look like without my shimmy."

Those words, although true, have nothing to do with this story. I write it only to divert your attention while I help myself to the last piece of pecan pie. Thank y'all.

Epilogue

Wadley, GA. 1949

Home Again

It was August in Georgia, hot and humid. I parked the rental car in the drive and stood, looking at a white clapboard farmhouse with green trim that had seen better days. A screened porch ran across the entire front, the screen an improvement since the days of my youth. On that very porch years earlier, I fanned gnats and shooed away flies. The hours I spent there playing, rocking, and swinging are innumerable. There was nothing remarkable about this place except it had served as a home for me and my family for sixty plus years. There is nothing particularly remarkable about my family, except that we made a good life there. Standing there looking at it quietly, I thought the old house looked as I felt after the long drive, tired and sad.

Two large cedar trees had once bordered the front yard. I had spent a childhood in these two trees and knew every inch of them. The larger one on the left had become a nuisance as some of the limbs had grown near the roof, and during a February ice storm, one had come perilously close to falling on the house. Dad eventually had that tree cut down, so there was only one left for my viewing on this day. I wish I had saved a piece of wood from that old cedar as a keepsake. No telling what memory the smell alone would bring back. The remaining cedar looked lonely with its partner long gone.

I looked to the left of the house where the garden had been, an area almost exactly an acre square, now sadly overgrown. Once vegetables grew there in perfectly laid out rows, a beautiful garden with green beans, red tomatoes, and yellow squash. Dad took pride with his garden, filled with everything a Southern garden should have. I pictured my Mother standing on the porch wearing a colorful apron with a paring knife in her hand calling out to me, "Allen, take this knife and a foot tub and get me a mess of okra for supper. Get one for your Big Mama, too."

I was old enough to cut okra and know the size of a mess. Though I was never thrilled with the assigned task, I replied, "Yes ma'am."

In the 50's "Yes ma'am" was the only acceptable answer. There was no sound this still August day, but I heard it, just the same.

I walked down the drive that led to the backyard, trying to take it all in, to remember. I passed under the magnificent magnolia tree that grew near the front corner of the house, providing shade for my parents' bedroom. I couldn't reach around its trunk with my arms and knew it to be more than one hundred years old. It was also the roosting place for the bantam chickens my father loved.

Next to the house sat a two hundred and fifty-gallon propane gas tank that supplied fuel to the space heaters warming our country home on cold winter nights. Near the backyard sat a mimosa tree friends and I had climbed, and beyond that a spigot. During my youth, no cooler drink could be found this side of a spring. The water would be made cooler yet if you let it run for a minute or two, as it was only a few feet from the pump house. I remembered an afternoon my uncle stopped by and wanted a drink of water, likely a similar humid August day with nights nearly as miserable. Up until that day the faucet faced downward making it hard to get a drink. He said to me, "Allen, you got a pipe wrench?"

I said, "Yes sir" and ran to fetch it.

He took the heavy wrench from my hands, fit it to the pipe and turned the faucet to face upward. I have never been so impressed in my life. A drink was much easier to come by after that. If he had been there on this day, I would have thanked him for the water faucet and for so much more. He had taught me to fish and ride a horse, although I was poor at both.

The pump house mentioned was a short cinder-block building, five feet high with a tin roof, a wood plank door and a dirt floor. I looked inside; all there was to see were a few boxes of junk. Fifty-five years ago you would have seen a neatly organized space: a well, a pump, a few hand tools, and if you looked really close, a pint of Early Times bourbon. Each evening Dad would have a drink and chase it with water. My Mother, a staunch Southern Baptist, did not permit such inside our home. Her faith aside, I don't think she begrudged her husband, a man of the soil enjoying a nip before supper, his reward for a hard day's work. When I came of age, Dad and I would enjoy the same on this very spot. What I wouldn't give to share another like moment and to see his appreciative grin for life's simple pleasures.

Twice I walked around the old house that August afternoon and recalled where another mimosa tree once stood, now gone. A white blossom dogwood was no longer there. I remembered games we children played; Kick the Can was a favorite. On the east side of the house we had played baseball; now the space seemed much too small for baseball. I could almost hear us kids laughing, us arguing, and Mama yelling for us to hush up. I could almost hear Dad's chickens crowing. I thought I heard a farm tractor, but it was a car coming down the paved road in front, a road that had been dirt during my youth. This car sped toward its destination, the driver never thinking that a young family once made a life in this old house.

I suggest that you go back to the home of your youth. There are lost memories to be found, and if you are as lucky as I, happy and good ones. Remembering and reliving is truly an emotional and heartfelt experience that brings tears to your eyes. It doesn't take long, but do it soon. Time gets away, and none of us knows in advance when it will be gone.

Acknowledgements

Thanks goes to those who helped make this book a reality...
Wadley photos courtesy of the website carrtracks.com.
Wadley High School photo courtesy of Alan Rachels.
Friends who supported me and those that helped.
Loretta Healy for cover design and formatting. Well done.
Judy Butler for editing. The book is a better read thanks to her.
Friends included here who allowed me to write about them.
My lovely sisters who allowed the same.
My parents, family members and friends gone too soon.
Know that you are missed.
And my wife Margie who loves me and makes me better.

www.ingramcontent.com/pod-product-compliance
Lightning Source LLC
Chambersburg PA
CBHW030322080526
44584CB00012B/674